T0099815

There's A Story In Every Box

Poems for Big Kids and Little Kids

Doc Lawrence

AuthorHouse™
1663 Liberty Drive
Bloomington, IN 47403
www.authorhouse.com
Phone: 1-800-839-8640

First published by AuthorHouse 3/29/2011

ISBN: 978-1-4567-4611-7 (sc)
ISBN: 978-1-4567-4610-0 (e)

Library of Congress Control Number: 2011903719

Printed in the United States of America

This book is printed on acid-free paper.

DEDICATION

This book is dedicated to the memory of my parents who infused our home with love, learning, and humor. It is also dedicated to my wife who has taught me the value and joy of a strong marriage. And to my children, who have enriched my life by allowing me to participate in theirs, thank you.

FOREWARD

My inspiration for writing this book of poems came about subsequent to hours of reading fun enjoyed with my children, particularly the poems of Shel Silverstein. My wife, who is a reading teacher by profession, wisely exposed our family to the world of children's and other readings. The influences for the poems came from friends, family, cultures, and personal experiences.

The intended purpose of this book was enjoyment for both reader and listener. What I did not expect was the great personal pleasure I derived from writing these pieces. I invite the reader to be as creative with the verbal delivery of these poems as he or she sees fit. The listener is likewise invited to be equally imaginative

The subject matter in the book is intentionally random, as are often the influences in our lives. The lessons in the poems are those that we choose to take away from the experience, as is also so often the case in our lives.

I would like to acknowledge the people I met along the way who offered insights and encouragement in the production of this book. Particularly David DiTullio, whose artwork brought vibrant life to a number of the poems.

Going forward, with a particular sentiment while reading this book, I would remind the reader of an expression: life is for the living. If one questions the meaning of this statement, asking does this mean for the people who can, or the people who would, or does this refer to the acts of living (intended or otherwise)? The correct answer is, life is for the living.

I hope you enjoy.

Sincerely,

Doc Lawrence

Contents

TELL ME A STORY

Tell me a story that I'd like to hear,
a story that makes me feel something.
A story so good that it holds my attention,
right up to the end that is coming.

If it's sad or it's funny or leaves me confused,
if it's clever and makes my mind bend.
Please read it to me. Then let's talk about it,
then read it all over again.

Perhaps we'll discover ourselves in the process,
or maybe just be entertained.
If you tell me a story, we both must contribute,
and grow just a little, for change.

THE TEE

Let me tell you the tale of a marvelous garment
that changed life for both you and me.
It's a story of struggle, of trial and error.
It's the legend that I call "The Tee."

Many lifetimes ago when people began
to cover up their derriere,
they figured out bottoms, without much a problem,
but for tops, well who knew what to wear?

So the clothes makers tried to create the right shirt
that would fit and make everyone happy.
Something comfortable and soft, something simple and easy,
that's casual but still could look "snappy."

Many styles were tried but none fared too well
as good qualities they all still did lack.
The fit was not good or the look was not right,
so their brains they continued to rack.

Shirts shaped like an A, shirts shaped like a K,
well you can't get too comfy in that.
Shirts shaped like a Y, one shaped like an I,
now how do you put on a hat?

The people tried B shirts and C shirts and D shirts
but none of them really did work.
Then G shirts and P shirts and V shirts and Z shirts,
to wear these could make you berserk.

It was Thomas The Taylor who Toiled and Tried
with The cloth That lay There on his knee.
He said "Hmmm" as he Touched it and "Hmmm" once again.
"What about The shape of a-
"Hmmm...?"

He knew we need comfort. He knew we want style.
The combination's Truly The key.
He picked up his needle and Thread and he said
"I Think That it should be a-
"Hmmm...?"

He said "Hmmm let us see, The shape That would be
a form where fashion and fit would agree."
"The answer's in me, Oh lord hear my plea,
just show me a sign That The shirt is a-
Hmmm...?"

Then his good wife Theresa said "Thomas Take Time,
sit down just relax and Then we
Together will solve This puzzle of yours
over Tasty biscuits and Tea."

"That's it" he cried out, "no more struggle and doubt,
the answer you've given to me!
Every woman and child and man that's about
would be happiest wearing a T."

The "T" was perfection. It felt just so right.
You could wear it all day, you could wear it all night.
You could wear it for bowling or swimming or school
you could look dressy or sloppy or look really cool.

And the people were grateful and filled with such joy,
they willingly offered a fee,
for this wonderful shirt whose fit did not hurt,
this new fashion that we call the "Tee."

Well, that is the tale as best I recall
in the manner as was told to me
So now you can see how we live so carefree
in a blissful T-shirt harmony.

MY FAVORITE CHAIR

My favorite chair is the one that spins
around and around and around.
I use my feet to propel myself
till I'm dizzy enough to fall down.

I love that it's soft and its pillows come off,
so I have it just as I like.
First thing in the morning it's the place that I go,
and just before bed every night.

It's my own special place where I sit with my bear,
it has comfort that we both prefer.
And if I get tired I might take a nap,
and drool on the chair and on her.

When I get a bump or a bruise or a cut,
it's a safe place for one little girl.
And if I feel sick, outside of my bed,
it's the place where I lie down and curl.

Each stain on it's mine and I think that's fine
and although it's cloth is now thinning,
I hope that as long as I live in this house,
I can have it and keep right on spinning.

WHEREFORE

Why can't you fill up a balloon with sand
and still have it float away?
Why can't the moon shine down on the land
and still be the middle of the day?

Why can't you go bowling with a ball that's square
and still have it knock down the pins?
And how come you never see chins on a hair,
and why won't a swimming pool swim?

Why can't you find a tree that grows cake,
so it could be picked fresh to eat?
Why can't you shovel snow with a rake
or use your nose to cut pieces of meat?

If the sky and the sea are both colored blue,
how do you tell them apart?
Why don't gummy bears live in the zoo,
and how come you can't see a fart?

I'm not sure why I don't have the answers,
and will they simply just come around?
Is all in the world just a matter of chance, or
is there knowledge I haven't yet found?

SMELLDIS

Bobby Shnozz would offer joy when it might come his way.
He'd hold a flower in his hand, and "smelldis" he would say.

A lemon or blueberry pie, a peach picked off the tree,
"smelldis" he encouraged as he held it givingly.

A freshly washed and dried T shirt, the ocean, and campfire.
He recommended "smelldis," so to share sweet sniff desire.

If you also enjoy good scent, wear the adventurer's hat.
But Bobby warns be careful to "smelldis and don't smelldat".

SHINE

Grandma says folks are like pennies,
millions of 'em circulatin' 'round.
Some are held precious, most are like others,
some lost and never been found.

She says "recognize that each one is special,
don't matter how old or how new."
They need handling with care, be they common or rare,
so they do well what all pennies do.

And that is to SHINE
when they're polished up fine,
just show them their rightful direction.
And brilliant they'll be,
they'll shine perfectly,
despite their unique imperfection.

POINT OF VIEW

When cowboy Slim rides into town
and leaves the dusty trail
he takes a bath, has a nice hot meal,
and then he gets his mail.
And after that he sees his friends
and visits with sweet Pearl.
After hard day's work, she cares for him,
you know that she's his girl.
She listens to his cowboy tales
and how much he is achin',
all the while she rubs his back,
with special care she's takin'.

But how about ol' Bo the horse.
Just what's my compensation,
for toting Slim upon my back
all over God's creation?
My hooves are sore, my tail is dry,
and what about my back?
I have to remain upon my feet
just to "hit the sack."
Do I get bathed, or fed fresh food,
or maybe get a letter?
I get cold hay, a stall to match,
and water, nothing better!

If you ask me Slim's got it good,
there's no complainin' he should do.
When cowboys say that life is tough,
consider the horse's point of view.

CAREER

Lindsay Jill at three years old would think about the folks she'd see. And wondered to herself, "Someday, when I grow up what should I be?"

Well, I could be

a mowlawner
a cuthairer
a sitterbaby
a manpolice
a makershoe
a farmerdairy
a catcherdog
a driverbus
a teacherschool
the fairytooth

She thought again about the choices. It came to her then, "Of course! First thing's to grow up and be an adult. You don't put the cart before the horse."

FINS

I saw a fish swim,
he turned on a whim,
I continued to watch in a trance.

Until I thought,
Hey his fins work OK,
but how does he zip up his pants?

MISS NANCY

I like Miss Nancy, she's my teacher.
She teaches me to play and learn.
She teaches me to use my words
and learn to wait 'till it's my turn.

She teaches us the ABCs
and also does the 1 2 3's.
And if I start to cry and whine,
she makes a sad face just like mine.

We paint with brushes
and draw with pens.
When she's not looking,
I paint my friend.

And if we make some cookies
that we form with our own hands
She makes us wash up just before,
so they don't taste like sand.

So I think I like going
when Miss Nancy teaches school
Who wouldn't want to learn and play
when fun's the firstest rule.

MAMA'S PICTURES

The picture collection on Mama's wall
showed the family members from short to tall.

They were hung in a fashion so one could view
each generation from old to new.

There were newborns whose heads had a little "peach fuzz".
There were old folks on whose heads we know hair once was.

There were little kids smiling with just their few teeth
There were some in neckties with clean shirts underneath.

You could see some with glasses that rest on the nose.
There were women in dresses, children lined up in rows.

There was brown, black, and blond, all colors of hair.
Four seasons of clothing, some babies were bare.

The picture frames varied in both shape and size.
And so did the people at times in their lives.

You could see the progression from child to adult.
And their own separate families that then did result.

And if pictures showed one person or twenty eight
they all marked a special time and a date.

So with each picture added and hung with such pride,
for the memories captured Mama laughed and she cried.

MANNY THE DETECTIVE

Manny the detective, he follows every clue.
To solve the current mystery, there's nothing he won't do.

Check fingerprints and footprints, to see which way they lead.
Get out the magnifying glass, to properly proceed.

It's careful work, detecting, even for the master sleuth.
But in the end there's great reward, in finding out the truth.

So he won't miss the subtle points and wrongly overlook these
answers to the riddle of where Mama hid the cookies!

FEAR

When I put my legs in my pants,
I feel secure, you know.
I watch as my feet enter,
and thereafter out they go.

And when my arms go in the sleeves of shirts,
I'm justified,
of comfort knowing that my hands
come out the other side.

But if I put my finger up my nose,
that is a scary trend.
Without an exit, who knows if
I'll ever see that part again.

CONFUSED

I'm sure that I can dress myself 'cause I know what to do.
There's hat for head, and glove for hand, and foot to fill the shoe.

But still one thing confuses, it's among my few pet peeves
What is a guy supposed to do with a necktie that has sleeves?

FAVORITE

I saw some mixed nuts at the store yesterday,
and I thought "If I had to pay for it?

Within the big mix, of all of the choices,
which one would I say is my favorite?"

There's peanut, Brazil nut and filbert you know.
There's cashew, pecan, and there's pistachio.

There's coconut, almond, and pine nut they sell.
There's walnut, and chestnut, and beechnut, as well.

So, if I had to choose amongst nuts big and small,
I think I like DONUTS the best of them all.

MANNERS

Formally greeting an octopus,
If his acquaintance, you should make.
Manners properly applied,
Which hand are you supposed to shake?

MO DON'T KNOW

If you ask Mo a question about the time, he'll tell you "Mo don't know."
Or how many pennies equal a dime, he'll still say "Mo don't know."
If you ask him a question about temperature he'll reply "Mo don't know."
Or the difference between a circle and square? It's simply "Mo don't know."
If you ask him, "Mo what makes up cheese?" Again it's "Mo don't know."
And does a tomato grow on trees? Same old "Mo don't know."
Would Mo know how to bake a bread? No way, "Mo don't know."
Could he keep directions in his head? Nuh-uh "Mo don't know."

But just you mention pizza and the smile on Mo's face grows,
for there he's quite the expert and there's plenty that Mo knows.

You throw the dough up in the air, for how long? That "Mo knows."
It goes in a pan that's circle or square, how thick? That "Mo knows."
The tomato sauce gets spread around, how much? That "Mo knows."
And the cheese is shredded, not finely ground, for certain that "Mo knows."
What different toppings can you get? Well all of that "Mo knows."
And exact cost of those things. You bet, precisely that "Mo knows."
The temperature at which it bakes, you guessed it that "Mo knows."
And just how much time will it take? To the second that "Mo knows."

His pizza knowledge knows no bounds, there's nuthin' Mo don't know.
But ask what's the next best thing he's found, he'll tell you "Mo don't know."

SHMORKY NOSE

When my friend Andrew gets a cold,
he needs to blow his nose.
'Cause otherwise the shmork inside
builds up and starts to flow.

Andrew needs to learn that if
his shmorky nose should drip.
He needs to use a tissue when
he wipes his upper lip.

And if that gooey greenish stuff
might come out with a sneeze,
it's not polite to raise your arm
and wipe it with your sleeve.

And when your tissue's all used up,
you throw away that "ick."
So when no one else is touching it,
then no one else gets sick.

So the next time Andrew has a cold,
with a nose all full of shmork,
I hope he gets a box of tissues
or if not, a pair of corks.

THE LOOKOUT

I'm looking out for ripplezips and nasty natchkebear.
I'm keeping watch for heskelunk and grizzly sobadare.
My eyes are kept wide open, 'cause you never know when there's
a chance one of those monsters might just catch you unaware.

So I'm prepared to keep awake and stay up all night long.
I'll do the job of lookout and I'll keep my vigil strong.
I'll spread the word on my patrol, if there should be some news.
As captain of the guard on watch, I know I dare not snooze.

But if by chance (yaaaaawn) one eye should close, and maybe then the other,
I'll have some time to (yaaaawn) rest myself, so then I can recover.
And when the job is to be done again tomorrow night,
I'll be fit and rested so that I can do it right.

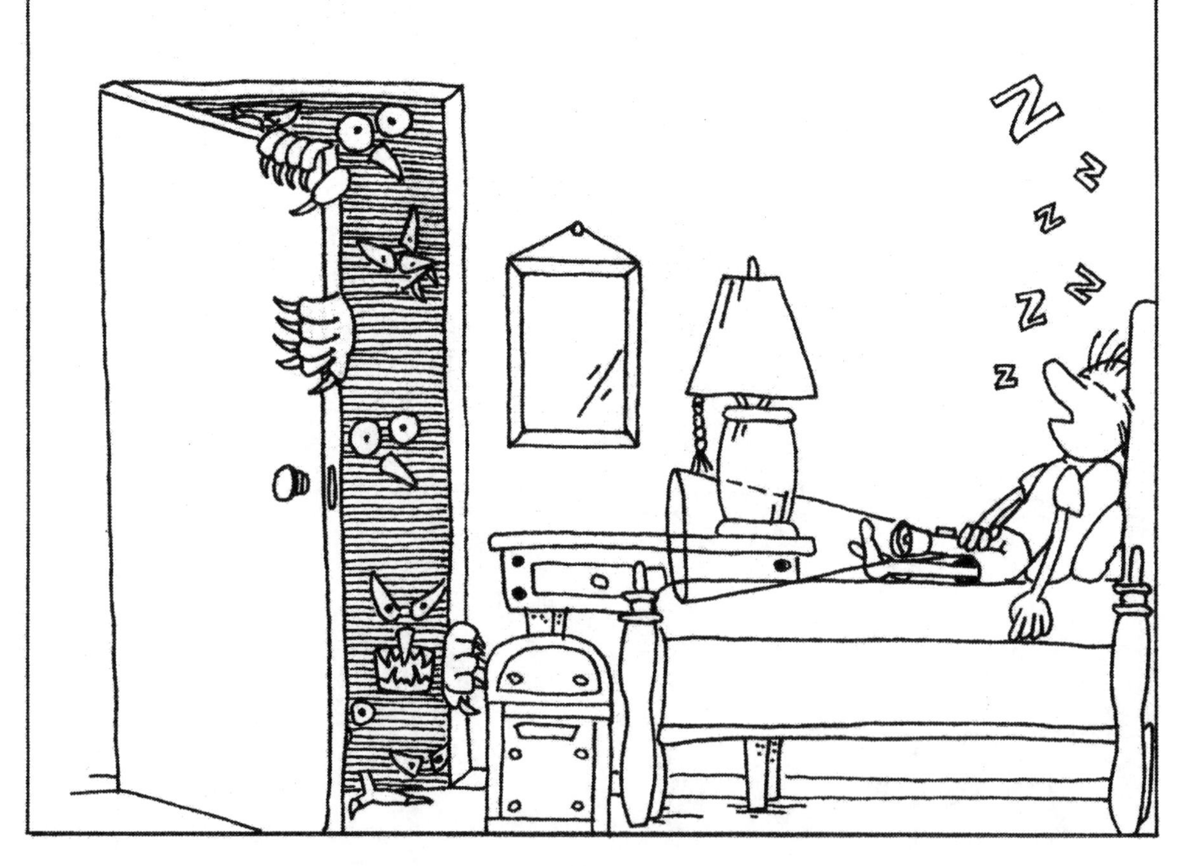

COLOR DAY

Know you all inside this house, it's yellow day today!
And that means planning meals in which you all can have a say.

But here's the catch, as you well know, the food must satisfy,
the color theme of dining today; now everyone say aye!

So, you there, you plan breakfast, and you will plan the lunch.
Then I will plan a dinner, and perhaps a snack to munch.

The first one said my breakfast will have grapefruit and an egg.
Bananas in some cereal, and that will start the day.

The second one said lunch will feature curried rice and buttered toast.
And then some pineapple or some peaches, whichever one you like the most.

Then number three said dinner will be chicken noodle soup,
along with corn and yellow squash, from the vegetable group.

And later in the evening if we watch two programs back to back,
popcorn is the obvious, to serve as yellow snack.

So now that you've been made aware that color day exists.
When ____________ day rolls around, what would be your menu list?

NOW AND THEN

Now and then, now and then,
it quick becomes remember when.

Then and now, then and now,
once body tall will take a bow.

So if you understand the how,
You'll appreciate that then is now.

THE WHISPER

The whisper's a delicate sound that you make, so only select people hear.

It's supposed to gently float through the air and, featherlike, fall upon ears.

It isn't supposed to be loud enough to travel terribly far.

It shouldn't be coarse and offensive like the sound of a smashing jar.

So remember when you start to whisper, your sensitive message begun;

It's meant to be spoken in hushlike tone, and not at the top of your lungs!

THERE'S A STORY IN EVERY BOX

I like to walk through the neighborhoods,
where I see all the homes in a row.
And I think of who lives there and what do they do,
and how do their daily lives go.

If there's one person, two people, three or fourteen,
there are common events to be heard and be seen.

There may be a dog, or a hamster, or cat,
or maybe an uninvited squirrel or a bat.

The smells of the food that they buy and they cook,
the style of furniture and how the walls look.

The books and computers and papers they read,
the things on their shopping list they think they'll need.

In some so much chatter, can't get in a word.
In some such a quiet, a sound barely heard.

In some they're so neat, they've completed each chore.
Some wouldn't know if they lacked a front door.

But the most interesting thing when I think of all that,
is considering how it would all interact.

In some when they get home they think how to play.
In some they think first "how do I get away?"

Of the happenings inside, beyond walls and locks,
if the house is of gold or of ill fitting rocks,
In my mind when I pick up each single rooftop,
I see there's a story inside every box.

W H A T

Wendell Williams Wittingly Wondered, Wherefore Would two people Wed?
Hector Hernandez Had Hidden His Hat; He Hoped it would Hop on His Head.

Allison Applebee's Attitude Alarmed All her Aunts by the Afternoon.
Tracy Tanada's Talkin' Till Tuesday and Totally Twisting a Tune.

Oh WHAT can this mean when random words play and seem to make no sense at all.
Oh WHAT then, so WHAT then, WHAT matters most here is WHAT's WHAT that's fun to recall.

NAMESTER

For the perfect name for my hamster,
I've truly searched the world over.
I thought I'd considered everything
from Abraham right up to Rover.
So here's a list of some names that I found.
I'm sure that I'll find the right one,
That I can say loudly, with love and great pride,
like he was my very own son.

There's:

Winston, Cecil, Nigel, Luke
Manuel, Paco, Jorge, Chico
Vinod, Deepak, Mahatma,
Muhammed, Ahmed, Hosni
Seji, Akira, Hiroshi, Hitoshi
Leif, Gunnar, Henrik, Sven
Ayotunde, Ifanyi, Simba, Tatendu
Chen, Mao, Yang, Yao
Wanahton, Takoda, Honaw
Alberto, Alfonso, Fausto...

Oh wait! There's just one detail
that I forgot to see to.
My hamster's a girl. Now everything's changed.
I guess now I'll just go with Sue.

DOODLE

Gina Vanetti took a bowl of spaghetti
and dumped it all over the floor.
She stared at the heap of wet pasta then thought,
"there's something here I should explore."

She started to lay out long strands in a row
that made up what looked like a street.
She then formed the outlines of several cars
that drove over pasta concrete.

The next group of pieces made the sun and the clouds
in the sky just above some roof tops.
And then she took pieces arranged in a pattern
that looked like a farmer's crops

She created buildings that looked like a city,
they went, maybe, ten stories high.
And she cut up small pieces to look like the birds
that would soar and then glide through the sky.

With the last of her pieces she fashioned some waves
that the wind on the lake was making.
And one little boat headed off toward the shore
near a street that the cars were taking.

When her Dad wandered in through the door to the kitchen,
he surveyed her floor pasta doodle.
Then he said, with great pride, as he took it all in,
"now that's what I call using your noodle!"

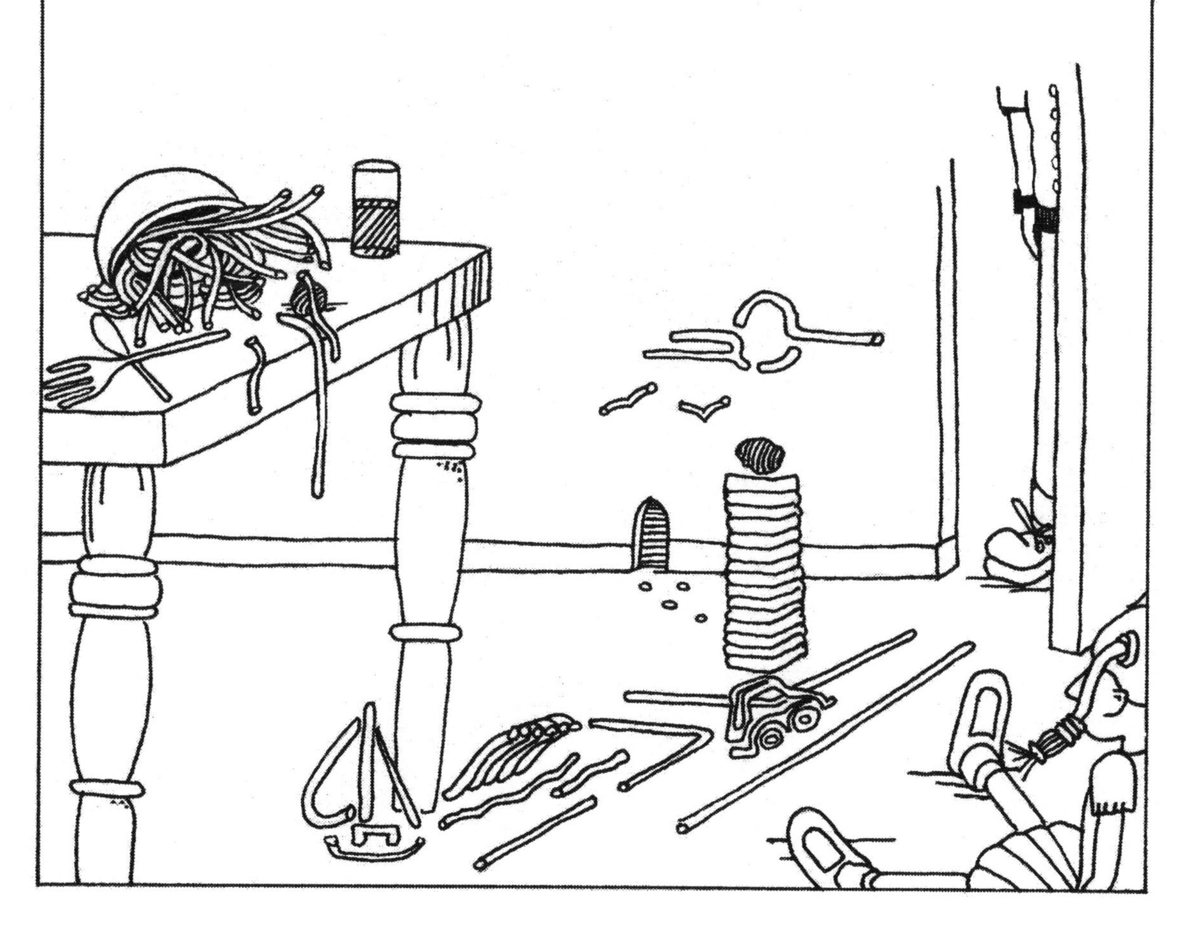

THE PERFECT COOKIE

The perfect cookie's not too hard,
but then again it's not too soft.
It cannot be so paper-thin,
nor have too much a lofty loft.

It has to taste so very good,
it makes you want another.
It has to be nutritious
so that it could please my mother.

The cookie must be storable,
so you could pack it, in your trunk.
The texture must be absolute,
so not to crumble when you dunk.

The shape can be negotiable,
oval, round, or maybe square.
And packaging would be in two's,
so when one's gone there's still a spare.

The bad news is today, so far,
all cookies I've had need correction.
The good news is I'll keep on tasting,
up until I find perfection.

DREAM

The other night it happened
that I had this vivid dream.
Everything had seemed so real,
in each and every scene.

And then there came this part
that did consume my very being.
I had this sense of comfort
and this image I was peeing.

So if someday you have discussion
about the real world's hint and clue.
Let me tell you this, my friend,
sometimes dreams really do come true!

DELICIOUS

I remember my mom in her kitchen, preparing food oh so delicious.
It was all so appealing, so memorable, and here are a few of the dishes:

pot pie in deep fry

calzone on the bone

tapioca on saltimbocca

octopus with baba gnush

egg roll on Italian brigiole

hot dog made from peanut log

egg foo young on deli tongue

lamb with ham on spam and clam

meats and beets on rice crispy treats

frosted flakes in my steaks, on pancakes

mellon that's smellin' and rotten au gratin

spumoni and bologna with connoli on stromboli

lemon salmon almond tart or peppers on a pastry heart

some mushy sushi fruit fajitas, chocolate radish cold carnitas

monkey that's funky in oil that's boiled, gruel that is cruel in tin that is foiled

Such tasty treats so unique and so rare, other moms could make dinner but none could compare.

Now I go out to restaurants, where they cook and they bake, but it's nothing at all like my mom used to make.

ATTITUBE

If a nabenan approaches you and offers you bezorg,
You tell him "Hey stot noffin, man! I'm no one's kippledorg."

"'Cause I don't do no rimbledimp, don't gimme that gishode.
You pack up all your binkledink, and boo-ya hit the road!"

THERE'S NOWHERE TO BUTTON THIS SHIRT

Young Ross stood at the bus stop.
He thought "I'm good and ready."
He wouldn't have thought otherwise,
not noticing things petty.

He brushed his teeth and dressed himself.
That readied him for school.
He packed his bag for lunch and class.
You know he's no one's fool.

Appreciating then,
all of his seven year old splendor,
I said to him,
"below your chin's a change that you might render."

He looked down somewhat skeptical,
as if to say "what for?"
He checked out shoes and pants and shirt,
what else is needed more?

For all he knew it worked just fine,
he's all fixed up complete.
Everything seemed in its place,
respective head to feet

So then I pointed out to him,
"Hey buddy take a look.
There's just one minor detail,
something simple you forsook."

And there he saw below his chin
a button stood alone
He surveyed once and twice again,
and then let out a groan.

"You see this button, there's no hole,"
he strongly did assert
"So if you can, just understand,
THERE'S NOWHERE TO BUTTON THIS SHIRT!"

"I'm not trying to be belligerent
and I wouldn't be rude or curt.
But take a good look and you'll comprehend,
THERE'S NO WHERE TO BUTTON THIS SHIRT!"

"THERE'S NO WHERE TO BUTTON THIS SHIRT!" he maintained
"THERE'S NOWHERE TO BUTTON THIS SHIRT!"
And as much as I gently tried to suggest,
his thinking I couldn't convert.

So I asked him again. "Are you sure there's nowhere?"
'Cause his feelings I don't want to hurt.
And he looked at me frustrated, as if to say
"you must be dumber than dirt!"

"THERE'S NOWHERE TO BUTTON THIS SHIRT!" one more time.
And I asked "are you sure this so?"
I showed him the hole at the bottom of the line.
He looked down then and simply said "Oh."

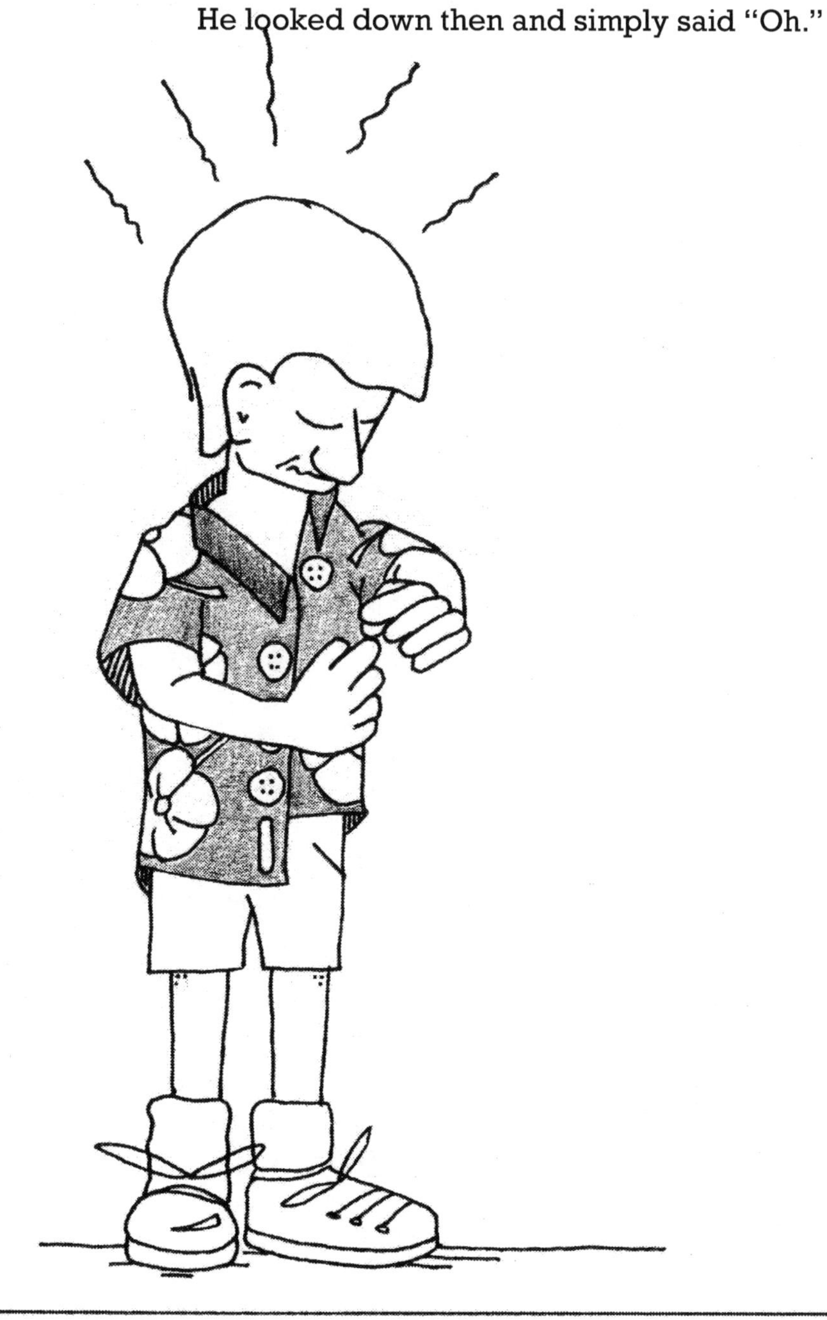

ALLIGATE

Perhaps I'm just a simple guy
I understand that a fly would fly.

Then, doesn't it follow, though I've never heard,
that practically, a bird would bird?

And if that's so, don't hesitate.
An alligator should alligate.

Well, shouldn't it?

JOOOOOOOEY

Jooooooey walks so slooooooowly,
he just don't seem to get tooooooo far.
Even when crossing the street at noon,
so's not to get hit by a car.

And Jooooooey talks so slooooooowly
that his words are aaaaaaall drawn out.
Even when something falls on his foot,
it's a minute till "ouch" he will shout.

When Jooooooey gets dreeeeeeessed it takes foreeeeeeever
to put on his clothes for the day.
Even when his friends call up and ask
if he can come out to play.

Jooooooey just doesn't do aaaaaaanything fast.
He seems like it all can wait.
I wonder, if we're now the same age, when I'm twelve
will Jooooooey be just turning eight?

WHINE

I'm tired of hearing "I don't wanna."
Don't give me that face looking sad.
You know if you say it again and again
I'll tell you, "that's really too bad."

And if you ask me one more time,
"do I really have to?"
I'll just be forced to say it once more.
"Yes you certainly do."

And should you go on again whining "why,"
that I'm mean and I always say no,
I'll tell you again the ultimate reason,
which is simply, because I said so!

I'm tired of you whining parents,
who don't accept obligation
I feel like my work as a kid's never done,
I can't take the aggravation.

I'm trying to make you responsible adults,
to be thoughtful, not full of neglect.
Sometimes I think that with parents, these days,
as a kid , I just get NO respect.

BOLD

"When I make a statement, I intend for it to be bold, decisive, and clearly understood. And that is how I intend to leave my mark in this world!"

"I see your point," said the paper to the pencil.

THE SEVEN HOUR SHOWER

When Tabitha takes a shower
it's almost a full day spent.
It's not just soap and water,
it's a full scale grand event.

Hour one is simple fun,
just splash and watch the water drop.
Hour two pretend to dive,
with cannonball and belly flop.

Hour three draw letters in
the steam that forms upon the wall.
Hour four is big league sports.
Pass and kick the soap football.

Hour five is soapy face.
Remove it with a finger shave.
Hour six is boats and ducks
that capsize in a tidal wave.

Hour seven, time to wash,
from ankles up to armpit.
And when a voice says, "you done yet?"
She answers "in a minute."

An hour then to dry and dress,
it's so nice to be able
to clean up in the morning
knowing dinner's on the table.

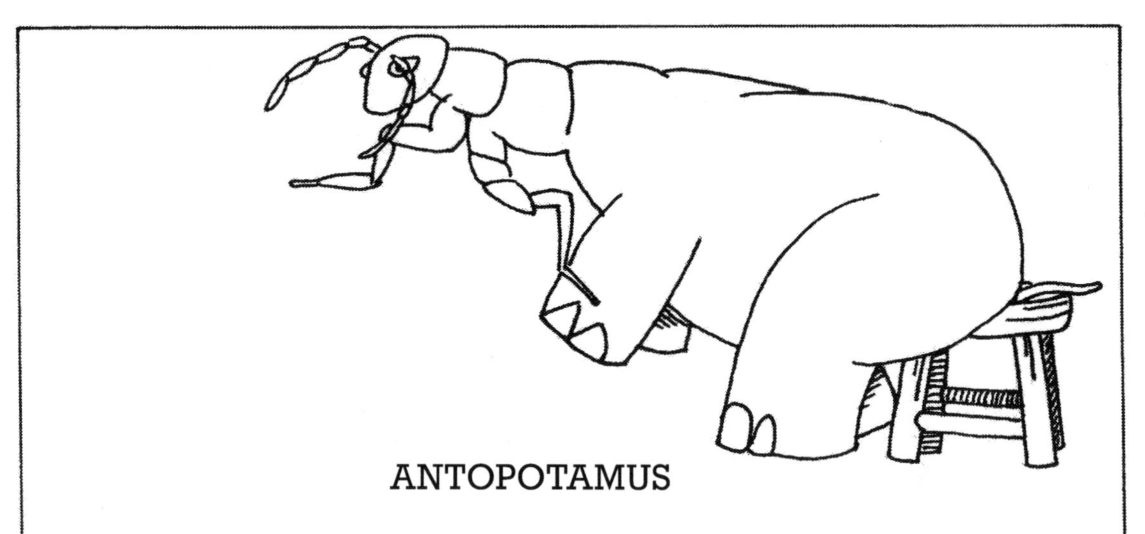

ANTOPOTAMUS

The antopotamus sits around
because it can't walk very far.
With tiny little front legs
and a butt the size of a car.
Antenna on its little head,
a tail on its backside,
a skinny little front end
and a rear end that's so wide.

It seems like such an awkward fit.
To me it makes no sense,
for such a mismatched front to back,
so small and so immense.
I never saw a stranger beast
that ever did pass by.
Except the time I chanced upon
a live rhinocefly

WHEN PIGS FLY

My Grandma has a saying
that she likes to use from time to time.
Like when Grandpa says that he'll remember,
she need not constantly remind.

Then she'll say something about some thing
drop her chin and raise one eye.
She'll set her hands upon her hips,
says "**that's** the day that pigs will fly."

If I think about the bird that pooped
upon my head and left me glum,
While I can't foretell the future,
I am hoping **that** day never comes.

NEW KID

"I'm the ruffest and the tuffest,
just because I am the gruffest,
and anyone don't like it, take a hike.
I'll fight ya brudda or ya mudda
and even any udda
of da people on ya street that I don't like."

"But, if you'll be my friend..................."

"I'm the sweetest, most completest,
nicest person who's indeedest,
just the bestest kid in town to have around.
I'm politest day and nightest,
and don't have to be the rightest,
in the comfort of the good friend that I've found."

ALPHABET ISSUES

The alphabet was not always
the happy sequence that you find.
There was a time when social divide
separated curves from lines.

The curves felt special, they were few,
being S, O, C, and U.
"We won't stand with lines in queue;
that we simply will not do."

And the lines like F, A, E, H, I...
L, K, M, and T, and Y,
said, "lines like N, V, W, Z
are the only kind that we'll stand by."

Well that left a third group of mixed appearance,
not perfectly curvy or lined.
B, D, G, J, P, Q, and R
had no happy place to find.

So those not pure of line or curve
were in between and did observe,
their allegiance was questioned. Where was their nerve?
And which group did they truly serve?

Well, time went on with much confusion,
an alphabet in disarray.
Until at last a voice called out;
the impassioned plea put forth by J

A, B, C, D, E, F, G?
H, I, J, K, L, M, N, O, P?
Q, R, S, T, U, V!
and W and X and Y and Z.

They looked amongst themselves
and then they soon began to see
that J was right, to stop this fight,
that went on needlessly.

So, A stood next to B
who in turn stood next to C
and D with E, then F and G,
and so on through to Z.

That's the day the voice of J
made differences smooth.
He taught acceptance of each other
as universal truth.

And so today that voice of reason
is the one that still commands
the letters of the alphabet
to cooperate and together stand.

SNOW DAY

I think that they should cancel school,
because of the weather today.
The T.V. showed Buffalo buried in snow,
and there's plenty more that's on the way.

The cars are all stuck and buses broke down,
the snow plows can hardly move.
The wind has whipped the snow around so,
in some places up to the roofs.

So I think that I should stay home today,
comfortable here in my jammies
That weather outside is freezing, you know.
So what if I live in Miami.

TALK AND DO

Talk and Do reviewed their states
and pondered their positions.
Each of them reflected
on their relative conditions

Talk says "That's what I always say" and
"I know that I oughta.
Yeah, I've a mind to get to it,
yep, I'm really gonna."

Do says "last one on my list,
that makes my work completely done.
My plan's accomplished, all's I need
is now to have some serious fun."

While Talk is busy yakkin' and is
fixin' to consider,
Do's on to the next thing, as the one before's
been signed, sealed, and delivered.

So when it comes to pick and choose
between both Talk and Do,
you might think about their outcomes
and decide which best suits you.

FLY

Old Mr. Green walked down the street.
His steps were made slow and with care.
He knew I was watching, as he made his way.
I tried really hard not to stare.

As he approached I looked up at him
and asked why he walked with a cane.
He said he got hurt, oh some time ago
and that made his right leg go lame.

Then I asked "what will happen if the left leg goes bad,
do you think you can still get around?"
He said "I can't see something so minor as that
altogether getting me down."

"You see son, this walking's a temporary thing,
and there's always a way to get by."
He motioned, come closer, then whispered to me,
"this is just till I learn how to fly."

HEAR

I said to Grandma, "I've a story for you. I'll tell it if you have the time."
She said "wait, let me put on my glasses first. Go ahead now I hear you just fine."

IF SNOWFLAKES WERE PEANUTS

If snowflakes were peanuts, how cool would that be,
with the sky dropping pellets of brown.
What would it be like, as it piled up high,
completely covering the ground.

Some melting would likely produce peanut butter,
a natural phenomenal feat.
Everywhere that you look would be the potential
to scoop up a spreadable treat.

All the lawns and the fields and the hills would be smooth,
and if that, on its own, might seem funny,
imagine the plows, snow throwers, and shovels,
all chopping and churning out crunchy.

But what about sledding, and boarding, and skiing?
That stuff is so thick you'd get stuck.
And you can't really walk or drive very well
trying to navigate that kind of muck.

The rooftops and trees would be dripping and sticky,
on your hat or your head the same thing.
And if you lay down to make a snow angel
you might get stuck and be there till spring.

So I have to consider this snowflake-peanut thing.
I guess that the notion's too strange.
But maybe, just maybe, with truck loads of jelly...
I wonder if that could be arranged?

INVENTOR

I wanted to be a great inventor,
make something the whole world can use.
To revolutionize the way we live,
and radically change don'ts and do's.

Something for both young and old
that will truly make our lives better,
an object known the world over,
the ultimate attention getter.

Of all the devices that we can have handy,
the thing that gets used every day,
that fits in your pocket and goes anywhere,
to be used while at work or at play.

In everyday life the thing most annoying
that drives almost everyone nuts,
is the fussin' and cussin' that goes along with
pulling underwear out of our butts.

So, I offer solution to what ails mankind,
no more need to squirm or to fidget.
A labor saver that keeps your hands clean,
I call it "the Wedgie Widget."

KLAVISH

Klavish the custodian's got a keychain full o' keys.
It's the monster bang collection, every kid at school agrees.
But none of us could figure out what all those keys were for.
The shapes and sizes looked like they unlocked more than just doors.

So one day me and Clifford Clay together got the nerve;
to question Klavish and find out what purposes they serve.
We asked him "Mr. Klavish, why so many keys upon the chain?"
He said "well now, I'm glad you asked, sit down and I'll explain."

"It's not your standard group of keys you simply hold and place in.
They're more like opportunities for all kinds of occasions.
There's rather an assortment here, to open things and make them close.
I can't remember every one, but I can tell you some to most."

"See this one here's for Mondays, so I call it the Monkey.
And this one's just for finishing up, so I call it the donkey.
When I'm takin' out the trash, that's when I use the junkey.
And if I feel like dancin', that's when I get out my funkey."

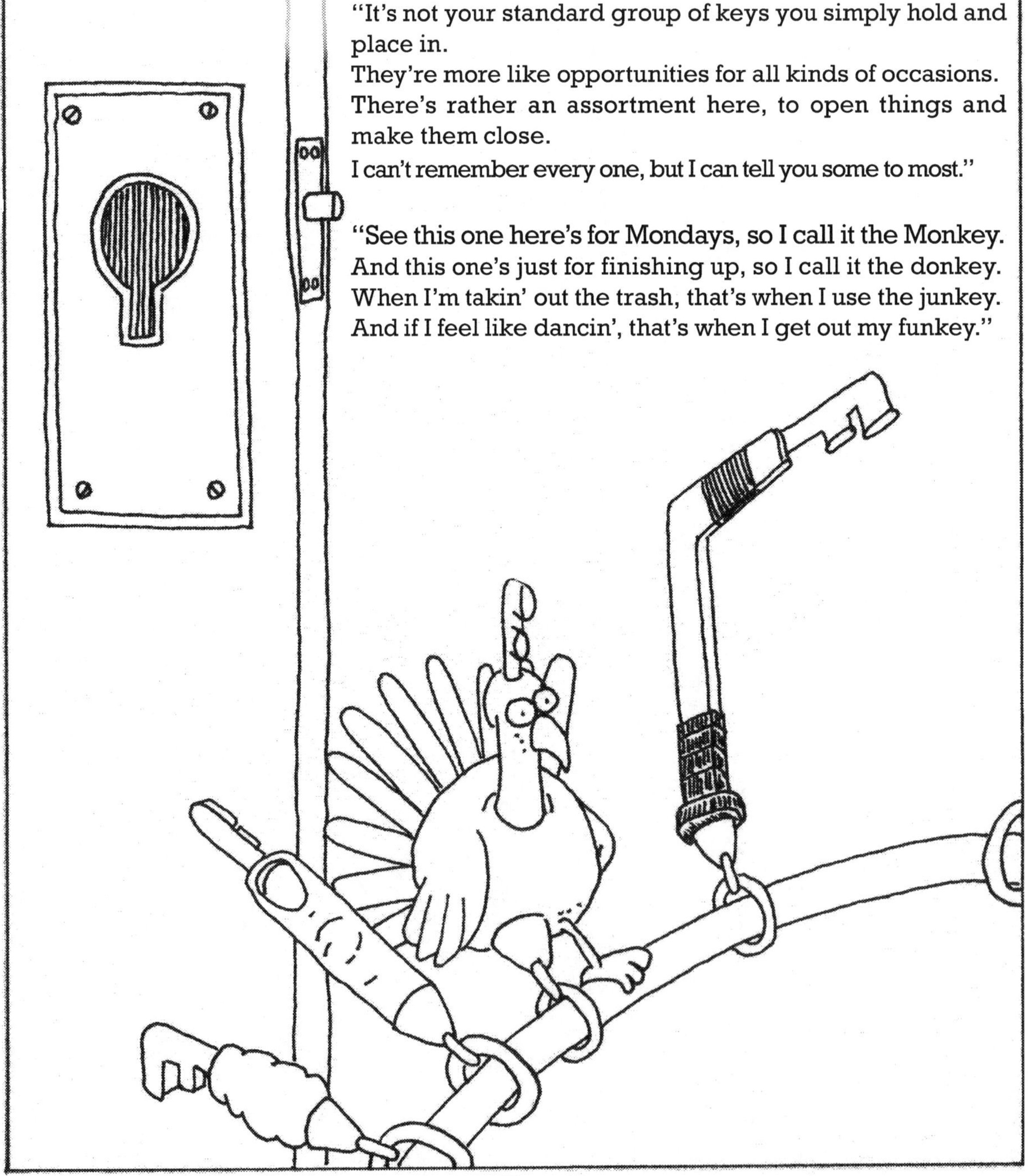

"If a ceiling's dripping in the closet, I open it with the leakey.
When I open doors with no one knowing, I will use my sneakey.
To enter stranger passageways, that may call for the freakey.
Opening chests of baby toys, for that I have a squeakey."

"For long and tall doors there's the lankey. Unhappy doors they get the crankey.
And doors I'm not too sure about, I'll use the hankey-pankey.
Slow doors get the pokey, funny ones need the jokey.
With doors aligned to work so fine, I use the okey-dokey."

"Doors with cloudy windows open easy with the murkey.
For doors that do not open smooth I have to use the jerkey.
Some doors that are a little odd might just need the quirkey.
And when Thanksgiving rolls around, well then it's time for turkey."

"If I feel like being rude, then I get out my porkey.
And if I feel I played the fool, then I deserve the dorkey.
For locks that are so easy, I need only use my pinkey.
And if I have some gas that day? You guessed it, that's the stinkey."

"I've got a stickey and a pickey, here's a shakey and a flakey.
A rockey, a hockey, a panickey, a riskey, a friskey, a finickey.
If I feel chance is on my side, then I'll break out my luckey.
And when I'm feeling brave inside, I'll utilize the pluckey."

"You see boys, these are special keys, their use requires some finesse.
There's study and hard work involved to find the key to your success.
And then some day I hope you will take on the one that's most demanding.
That my friends we call the key to love and understanding."

STARS

There are moments late at night
when I'm looking up at the sky.
And it seems to me it's not quite as bright
and there's disbelief in my eye.

I'm so used to seeing the stars in their place
and lately I'm missing a few.
For the brilliance they shed seems to have fled
and now I must think this thing through.

In my life there were stars that were bright in the sky
to show me the heaven's direction.
Their guiding light showed me which way was right
and offered up cosmic connection.

I assumed they would always be there for me,
as sometimes they lost my attention.
So how could they dull, negating the lull
that they'd always shine on by convention.

Now I can't understand that the light shines no more.
It's too hard to comprehend why.
Are they there just the same? Is my vision to blame?
Or did they simply fall out of the sky?

LITTLE JUSTINE THE TISSUE QUEEN

Little Justine the tissue queen
lamented her sad situation.
It's been seven long days and her cold is still there,
And it's caused such severe consternation.

"Ib beed coughig ad sdeezig ad blowig by dose
Oh dis really is biserable sdadus.
Sobetibes if I hab fibe sdeezes togeder
De lasd wod's so hard I ged fladus."

"Ad by dose jusd keebs flowig so derefore I'b blowig
ad wipig wid tissues all day.
I cad wade to go oud ad play wid by freds.
Oh wed will dis code go away!"

Well the good news is ten days have passed altogether
and Justine is one quite happy kid.
She says "dobody dows just how rotted a code is.
But I dow ad I do ad I did."

THE PITCHER ON THE WALL

My mom said I need some refining,
that I need to learn more of the arts.
And listen to opera and see the ballet
and use language that makes me sound smart.

She said "sports cannot be all that you do,
it's time to expand your horizons."
Football, basketball, soccer, and hockey,
"you need culture to focus your eyes on."

So we went to the art museum
to see all the cultural works
of some of the great civilizations,
like the Romans, the Greeks, and the Turks.

We saw sculptures and weaving and pottery pieces,
there must have been seventeen halls,
with lines on the floor showing which way to go
to see paintings that covered the walls.

At first I thought this would be boring,
with all the art work in the building.
But once I saw paintings and forms showing sports,
well that is when I became willing.

There were wrestlers and horse riders, guys throwing spears
and champions of all ancient sports.
And modern art showing baseball and football
and kings of the basketball courts.

So when Mom asked me if there was something I liked
I said "yeah." She corrected me "yes."
She said "tell me, your favorite piece of art work."
I said "it's a painting, I guess."

I told her about a painting I saw
of a baseball player I didn't know.
He was wearing a Baltimore Giants shirt.
He was winding up for the throw

And I thought he looked focused, intent on the game,
his face showed competitive state.
His body was coiled up, ready to launch
a fast ball right over the plate.

"Yeah, that's my favorite, the best that I've seen,
I like the pitcher on the wall."
"Its picture," she said, and "yes" she corrected.
"Don't let your grammar fall."

"Yeah that's what I said" as I raised up my head,
"the pitcher is really exciting."
She said "picture" again and "yes" again
with a tone of voice some might call biting.

"That pitcher is somethin'," I said with conviction.
"I now look at art with contentment."
"Its picture" she hissed "and that's something" she said,
but yet I was sensing resentment.

"You know," I told Mom, "you talk a good game
about how you take culture to heart,
but your attitude says you just don't have patience
to appreciate really fine art."

ANAGRAM

I thought that I'd impress my dad with ability to spell.
I'd show him hidden secrets of some words that I knew well.
"You see Dad if you look real close and turn the word around,
a different word discovered and new meaning there is found.

See:

Raw is war and god is dog and tap is pat and top is pot
And pin is nip and ram is mar and leek is keel and ton is not."

He looked and shook his head as if to say yes I agree.
But, practical man, he took his stand and said "this, you really should see.
While you've opened my eyes to recognize the depth of this word group
No matter how you cut it son, poop is still just poop."

MAKE WISHES ON FISHES

Make wishes on fishes and watch them go round
as they flash and they float without but a sound.
See them swirl all together and then separate,
as would the intent and directions of fate.
And then when you tire of tracking their course,
know that sincerity bears no remorse.

ARE WE THERE YET?

"Are we there yet?" I asked in the first twenty minutes
that Mom started driving the car.
"Are we there yet?" I said after twenty five minutes.
I thought that we'd driven so far.
"Are we there yet?" again, within thirty five minutes.
"Are we gonna sit here all day?"
"Are we there yet?" once more, I wanted to know,
"are you sure that we're going the right way?"

"ARE WE THERE YET?" I hollered then Mom stopped the car
and gave me a frightening look.
But before hollering back in an angry voice
'twas an extra moment she took.
She stared out the window, not saying a word,
collecting the thoughts in her head.
And when she turned 'round she looked happy and calm,
and these are the words that she said:

"Are we there yet?" you ask, you must not understand,
we can never truly be there.
For once we get there, then there becomes here,
and of this I'm sure you're aware.
If there becomes here and where we are becomes there,
and we can only ever be here.
Then here was a there and there is now here.
Now that should be perfectly clear."

I have to admit, that I just had to quit
asking my question again.
I'm just so confused and really not used
to here and there making no sense.
I know I was here and wanted to get there,
and that was the travel design.
I guess now I've learned that we'll never get there,
I just hope that we make real good time.

ERIK THE RED

The history books speak of Erik the Red,
the Viking voyager warrior.
But little is known about the hair on his head,
it was his beard he was largely known for.

What historians lack is a clear understanding
of how his fierce look came to be.
Those of us who know best are delicately handling
the answer to that mystery.

He was first recognized, as his burly beard grew
originally as Erik the Brown.
From his appetite for tasty, down home barbecue,
and the sauce on his beard that dripped down.

As the years did pass and his tastes took a change
he was a hot dog and mustard fellow.
That altered the color of his broad facial mange.
And thus there was Erik the Yellow.

As time passed on his manners declined.
And he hankered for French fries instead.
With a boat-load of ketchup to drip as he dined,
he then became Erik the Red.

By the end of his travels, his fame had spread wide.
He was Erik the Red, and here's why,
his years exhausted, he eventually died
just before tasting blueberry pie.

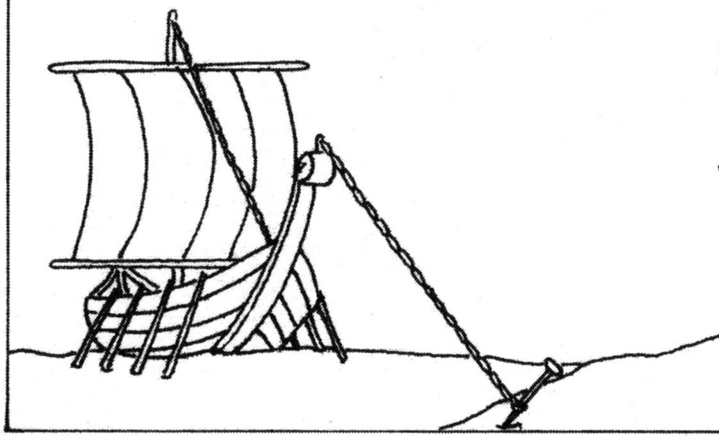

PIERRE VOCALAIRE

Pierre Vocalaire's a professional singer
he works at the local café.
He enjoys the work he does three nights a week,
and delivers newspapers by day.

'Cause sometimes, you know, the singing work's slow,
if the café tables aren't very full.
And it's not always easy, making a wage,
with the accordion's push and a pull.

But Pierre's a smart fellow, who knows his own strengths
and how to appeal to the crowd.
He can't really play or sing all that well,
but he knows to perform rather loud.

For the high notes he'll hit, patrons cringe and may grit
their teeth or cover their ears.
He knows if he plays a long melody,
it can move happy couples to tears.

So after a sour note he might strike, he says "Madame and Monsieur if you like,
I'll stay here and finish my tune.
Or if you prefer, your music deferred.
Buy a song for your friend 'cross the room?"

And so back and forth Pierre goes all night,
serenading and offering joy,
especially to those who sponsor others
by paying the musical boy.

NAYCHUR DUZZ

I know a man, lives in the hills;
his name is Naychur Duzz.
He doesn't waste a single thing,
he says that it's because

That which humans utilize
will have its day and use will pass.
And if we want our world to be
so that it will forever last

We must recycle and reuse
and take care that we don't pollute.
Regard the laws the earth has taught,
both evident and absolute.

So if we want a world in which
we're going to get from that which was
We'll treat resources with respect
and do as Naychur Duzz.

BOOMERANG JACK

Boomerang Jack learned his skills
in the outback of Australia.
His teacher told him "if you want to have
a talent, that'll never fail ya.
Then *throw* each day so eventually
you'll become a natural, Jack.
And then when you *throw*, you'll have no worries,
you know it'll always come back."

So all his young life Jack practiced
the *throwing* of the boomerang.
He developed his skill so it always came back,
you could say he had gotten "the hang."
With each single wind up and "give it a *throw*"
it was guaranteed to return.
Jack had mastered the fine art of *throwing*,
knowing most all one could learn.

Now you'd think that such a talented man
wouldn't have any problem to face.
But actually for Jack, with all that he knew,
well sometimes that wasn't the case.
For knowing so well how to master the *throw*,
in the manner of a boomerang man,
created a whole new set of problems,
for which Jack hadn't quite planned.

He tried to play baseball but that didn't work,
'cause each time the ball would get hit,
he would grab that ball and give it a *throw*,
but it wound up back in his mitt.
He tried *throwing* horseshoes in competition,
making "ringers' around the steel stake.
When that piece of iron came flying back at him,
that Australian was one worried mate.

Once for his best friend's birthday,
Jack *threw* him a huge party bash.
But each of the guests that attended
gave Jack all the gifts and the cash.
He'd *throw* out the garbage, just like his neighbors,
in accord with the township plan.
But week after week, all trash collected,
his kept coming back to the can.

He once *threw* a fit and just what you'd think,
that attitude came back his way.
He *threw* his hat in the ring to participate,
but you know that the hat didn't stay.
And when he *threw* caution to the wind,
the wind brought caution right back.
There were times when he *threw* himself into his work.
Work *threw* back a frustrated Jack.

So Jack thought to himself, "self, what is the matter,
why should the problem be,
that every literal and figurative *throw*
results in return back to me?"
And then in a flash it all became clear,
"I'll show this phenomenon who's boss.
From now on absolutely no more *throwing*.
I'll just give a little toss."

SUPERMAN

Superman the man of steel,
his body's indestructible.
He can't be burnt, or cut, or broke,
even his hair ain't crushable.

So, if he's that rough and tumble,
and his body never fails,
what's the poor guy gonna find
that'll cut his fingernails?

STREAMING

Row, row, row your boat.

'Cause it won't go where you want, unless you do.

TALKIN' TED

Talkin' Ted can talk all day,
'bout anything he knows.
You simply name the topic
and away the chatter goes.
He can talk about the weather
and the color of the sky.
He'll then go on to talk about
the type of clouds and why.

If you think you know history
or government or law.
Ted knows more stuff. He's done more stuff,
and seen more than you saw.
He knows the cultures of the world
and many foreign lands.
And famous people, what a list,
with whom he's shaken hands.

And Ted knows every vegetable
and flower, herb or weed.
He'll happily go on at length
'bout root, or bulb, or seed.
He knows all of the planets
and knows all the constellations.
A stellar conversationalist,
he'll start with the creation.

If you need some advice on how to sail a boat or build a house,
if you want every detail 'bout the creatures from the whale to mouse,
if you are seeking knowledge, what's the universe about?
If you want all the answers from the source that has no doubt,
if you might have some time to spare, just an hour, or a year.
Ted won't ask much of you, I swear, if you will lend him your left ear.

JIM NASTIK

Jim Nastik's fantastic. He flies through the air,
as he shows off his athletic stunts.
He's so acrobatic, performs automatic,
so graceful, and nary a grunt.

He can do half a gainer and make it look plainer
than sitting and filing your nails.
He contorts all his limbs, dipsy-doodles again,
As he elegant through the air sails.

But his coach is concerned, and he hopes Jim will learn,
the most polished way down to the mat
is to finish the dismount with a "stomp" on his feet,
instead of his face with a "splat."

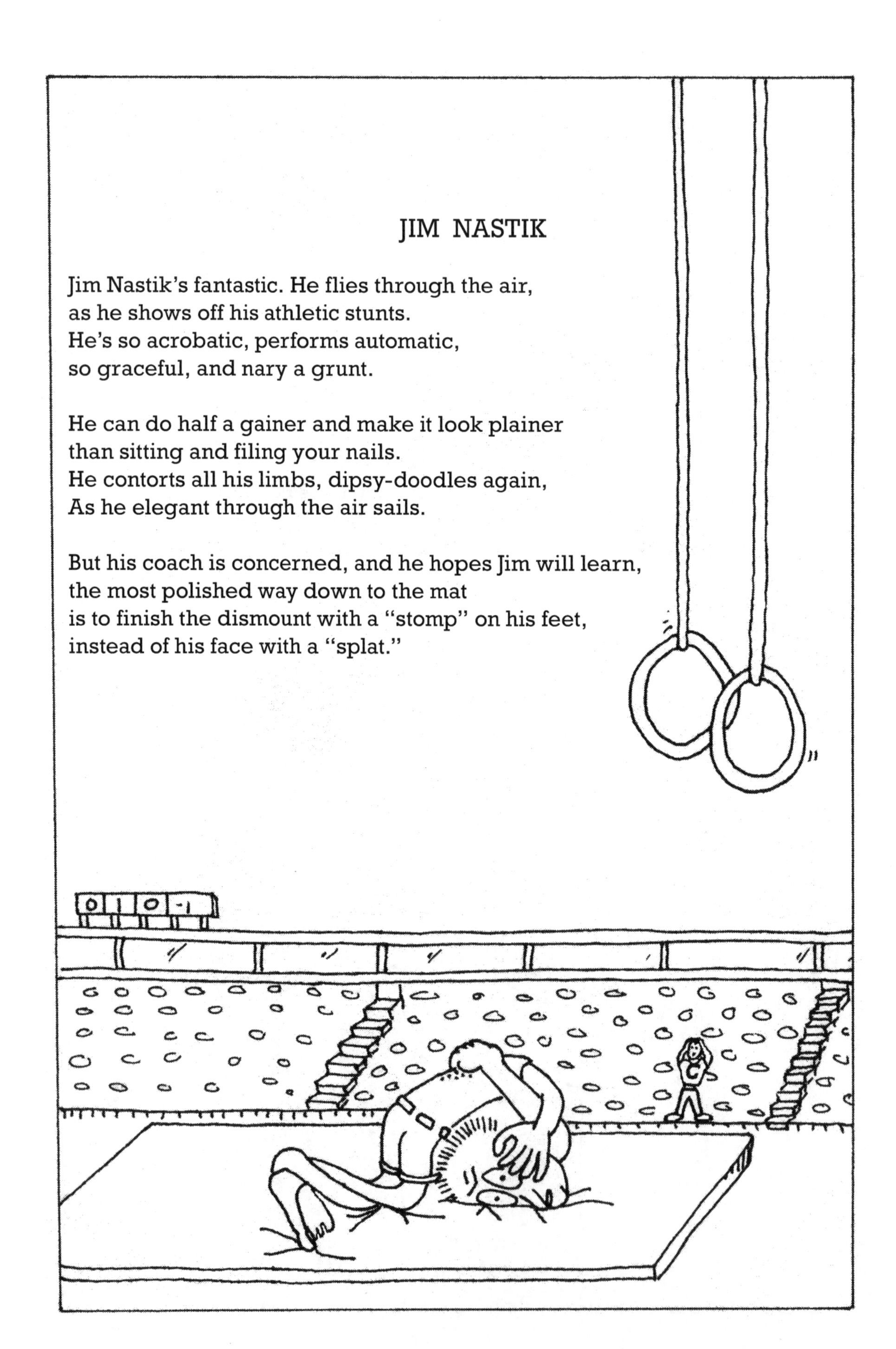

CELL PHONE

I got this brand new cell phone,
and it does some real neat stuff.
It calls and texts and calculates,
and if that aint enough.
It'll take a picture, play a song,
and act like a computer.
It buzzes, burps, and giggles,
and makes noises even ruder.
And Dad says when I wear it on my ear,
to which it clings,
it lends a whole new meaning
to the concept of ear- rings.

IF YOU KICK A CAN

If you kick a can from here to Japan,
and then covered most of all Asia,
you'd cross every country that ends with a "stan;"
then China, Nepal, and Malaysia.

In Africa you could go kickin'
from Egypt to Niger to Kenya.
A left at Angola, a right to Botswana,
straight to South Africa and then ya
kick to Cameroon and then pretty soon
there's Ghana, Burundi, and Chad.
You could pogo to Togo, and elsewhere, I don't know.
But I bet there's yet more to be had.

When you kick to Australia, there's a whole lotta land.
There's Fiji, New Zealand, Samoa.
And then if you wanna you kick through to Tonga,
and that's all Australia I knowa.

In Europe, the kickin' just goes on forever,
through Poland and France and Armenia.
Go well past Croatia and right thru to Iceland.
The Greeks and the Swiss will be seein' ya.
Keep kickin' to Russia and Denmark and Sweden
and kick right on down thru Norway.
And then there's a place for Ultimate Kickin'.
I think that's what meant by U.K.

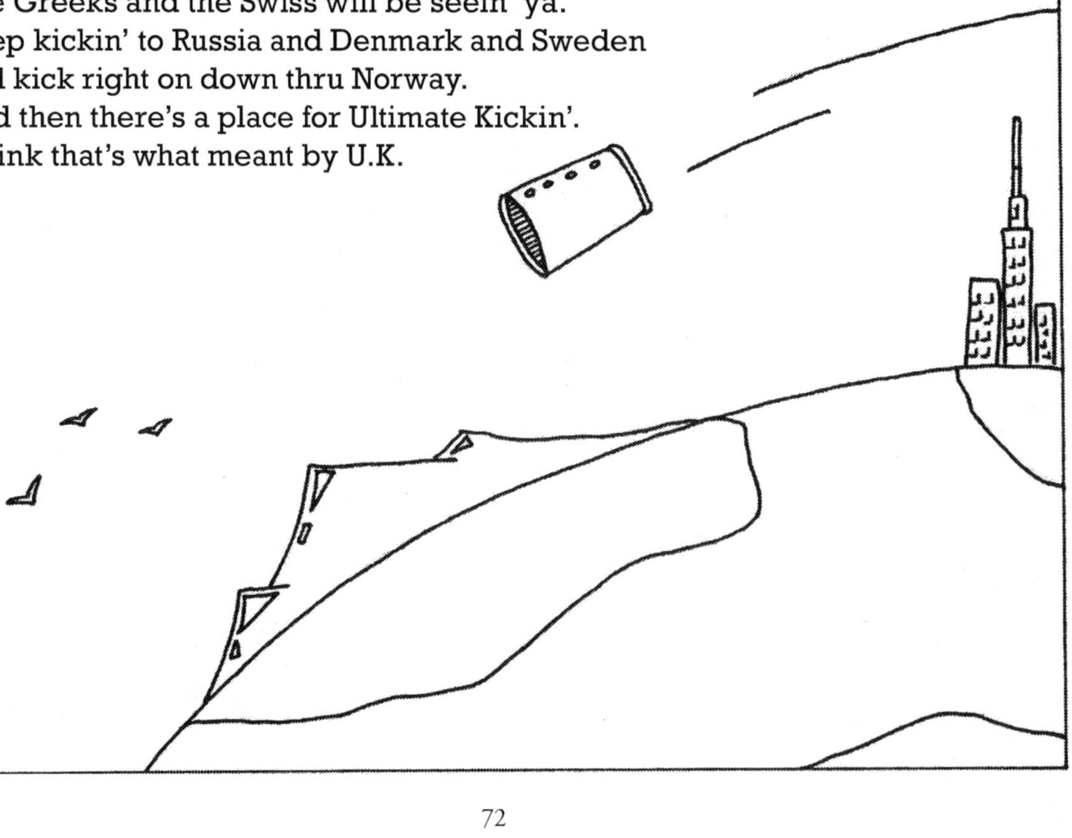

Kickin' up then South America's way,
there's Chile, Brazil, and Peru.
Uruguay, Ecuador, Venezuela.
You could kick thru Columbia too.

In North America there's miles o' kickin',
from Nicaragua to Belize.
Canada, Mexico, United States,
where the can kickin's just as you please.

Now, if you can't travel all over the globe,
'cause money or time is restrictin'.
Sit back, close your eyes, and think where to go,
and then in your mind, just start kickin'.

SCOTTY McDOTTY

Scotty McDotty went to the circus, with all of its fanfare and show.
The acrobats swung and twirled overhead and the animals did tricks below.
As he sat in his seat and watched it take place, he thought "that doesn't seem very hard."
With each next performance he said glibly and loud, "I could do that in my own back yard."

So, after hearing this quite a few times, the ringmaster took off his hat.
The frown on his face was becoming a smile, when all of a sudden, like that
He looked at the tigers. They looked back at him. He glanced at the monkeys and clowns.
The seals and the horses and elephants winked, knowing what was about to go down.

The high diver left his platform and the lion tamer put down his stick.
The circus men set up more chairs in the ring, things were taking shape quick.
Two circus jugglers went into the crowd and lifted the boy from his seat.
They carried him over the steps to the ring and placed him down on his feet.

The ringmaster said "We've been listening, young man, to your comments and boastful rants.
We've decided to make you the star of the show, with a once in a lifetime chance.
You can prove your mad skills and show everybody exactly how this gets done.
All eyes are on you; the circus is yours. Well, go ahead and show us, son."

Scotty climbed up the ladder to the trapeze on high as the lions and tigers lay down.
And he stepped on the platform ready to jump. The audience did not make a sound.
The drum roll began as Scotty got ready to make his first daring leap.
The elephants and clowns bought peanuts and popcorn and parked themselves in their seats.

Scotty took off on the swinging trapeze; his partner prepared for the catch.
But Scotty didn't swing far enough and missed. The crowd had let out a gasp.
He fell toward the floor, was saved by the net, and flopped around like a fish.
The elephants judged and scored Scotty's big dive, out of 10 none gave more than a 6.

Next Scotty went to the big cats cage where he jumped from stand to stand.
The lion tamer hollered and cracked his whip and smiled at the cheering fans.
Scotty said "I'm jumpin' as high as I can, be careful with that whip."
The worst was when the tamer forced Scotty's mouth open and tried sticking his head in it.

For the next circus feat Scotty was juggling, he was handed six wooden pins.
The monkeys decided they liked this act the best, so they clapped and showed off their grins.
Scotty got three wooden pins in the air, so he then went to throw the fourth one.
When pins began dropping on his feet and his head he realized that wasn't much fun.

He tried walking backward on balancing balls, like elephants do, and he found.
That it's not as easy as they make it look, and your butt hurts when it hits the ground.
He tried to do flips like monkeys and clowns, the seals clapped with appreciation.
More often than not he fell on the floor and learned about circus frustration.

Now the ringmaster said "Have you learned something son, about circus-performing acts?"
Scotty said "Yes. I've a whole new perspective, and here are the simple facts."
Scotty said "this is more than I can handle. I'm tired, and I'm bruised, and I'm beat.
I now know my place in the rings of the circus, and I'm going back to watch from that seat."

MISUNDERSTOOD

It's me shoeses that chooses to take pirate cruises
'cause I'm really a land lubbin' lad.
And me sword that's aboard, makes ill gotten reward.
It's not me that's behavin' that bad.

It's me coat that's cut throat on this boat that's afloat,
on a sea of misfortune and crime.
And me belt that's what's dealt a few red stingin' welts
on me crew that's the dregs of mankind.

If me pants gets a glance at a thieverin' chance,
then you know there's no holdin' them back.
And me hat's what's begat livin' like a ship rat,
'cause me head wouldn't think to do that.

They say clothes make the man, and you see what I am.
The appearance is that I'm no good.
But the truth is I'm couth, not one dishonest tooth.
It's me looks makes me misunderstood.

????????????????????????????????????

"Who do you think you are?" she asked.
I really didn't know what to say.
"When are you going to learn?" she shrieked.
I thought about that one all day.

"How many times have I told you?" she wailed.
I counted until I was tired.
"Do you think the world revolves around you?" she moaned.
I thought, heavenly science – required.

"WHAT IS THE MATTER WITH YOU?" she cried.
And that really rattled my brain.
"Well, I'm waiting," she said with a frustrated huff.
When finally I had to exclaim,

"These questions are so complex" I said,
"it takes years for knowledge to grow!
You're the adult in this relationship.
So, **you** tell me how should **I** know?"

WILD BILL WOOSTER

Near the city of Nashville, a van rolled up
to a stop at a neighborhood curb.
As the driver stepped out he surveyed the house,
his boots on the pavement were heard.

He tipped back his Stetson for a good second look.
He was getting the lay of the land.
He patted the heads of the children he saw,
tipped his hat again, said "Howdy Ma'am."

"From the looks of things, this here ranch needs some 'tending,
got a problem varmint mob."
He pulled up his belt and said "I'm just the cowboy,
for this kind of roundup job."

"Them roaches like grazing where the food crumbs are plenty,
with the occasional soft drink spill.
They hang out in cupboards and drawers in the kitchen,
till they're opened, then run for the hills."

"And they ain't just pesky, them swift movin' critters,
they multiply if they ain't caught.
Along with the nuisance, and maybe diseases,
they'll eat all the food that you bought."

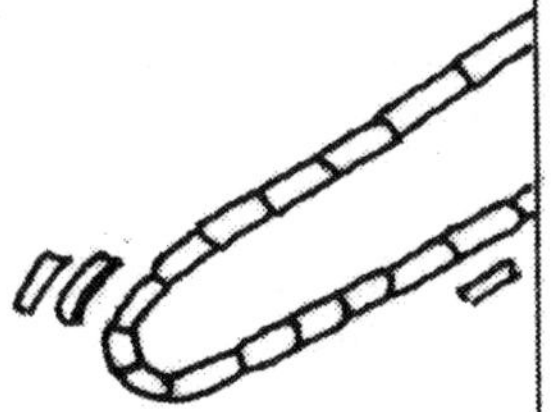

"If you let 'em run wild and roughshod 'round here,
they'll come and they'll go as they please.
What you need's one tough caballero, my friend,
who corrals cucarachas for fees."

"I'm Wild Bill Wooster" he said with a smile.
"And I'll fix up your problem home.
I'm a cowboy exterminatin' son of a gun,
and I ride where the cockroaches roam."

"So, excuse me now, while I saddle up Silver,
my partner and trusty steed.
Step back buckaroos, as the herd dogs come through
there's gonna be a cockroach stampede."

Now Silver was truly the color of the name,
a bullet shaped canister rocket.
As Wild Bill saddled up Silver he rolled out
the bullwhip attached at his pocket.

Then three prairie dogs scampered in behind Bill,
and took up their ready position.
"Git along little doggies" he said to his crew
"let's head out and do us some riddin'."

"Yeeeeeeeee Haaaaaaaaa!" he screamed, as he cracked his whip
"I'm a wranglin' cockroach raider!
We're gonna clean up these parts and ride through this house
in a whirl, like a western tornader!"

He hopped in the saddle and Silver took off,
pretty much like a rocket, you'd say.
They shot up the upstairs and shot down the downstairs,
leaving behind an odd spray.

So for maybe an hour you could hear Wild Bill holler,
crack his whip and drop pellets like hail,
until he and Silver had come to a stop.
He said "this here's the end of the trail."

He looked at his dogs and asked "ready boys?
Any minute that herd'll come through."
Lining both sides of hallway that led the way out,
they barked knowing well what to do.

Then after a few more moments of quiet,
came a rumbling kind of sound.
It continued to grow, getting louder and louder,
like the thunder of hooves on the ground.

Well the walls started shaking and the family got nervous,
and Bill said "best stand out the way.
When I open that front door all heck's bustin' loose,
gonna run for the light of the day."

Wild Bill turned the handle, got himself ready,
sidestepped and flung open the door.
Then faster than you can say "jeeeumpin' catfish"
the stampede began with a roar.

They ran from the bathroom and bedrooms and kitchen,
the dogs barked, directing the flow
to the bug corral, a great big container,
Bill set at the door's edge below.

When all of the roaches had tumbled inside,
Bill quickly threw on the lid.
He tied it all up with his lassoing rope,
making sure of the tie up's tight fit.

The three dogs and Silver hopped into the van,
covered in trail-riding dust.
Bill packed the container, along with his saddle,
and the rest of his bug roundup stuff.

"Well, that about does it" he said to the woman,
"that's the last you should see of them pests."
"Me and my posse'll be takin' our leave,
and probably head for parts west."

"I'll hitch up the wagon, and be on my way,
gonna follow the western sky.
Guess I'll keep on ridin' till that last cockroach roundup."

Don't that bring a tear to your eye?

CHEF'S ADVICE

Every day the same old thing;
there's no variety in your choice.
Your dietary habits have you
speaking in one single voice.

It's a big wide world that offers you
experiences for your tongue,
with lots of cultures in the mix
that you may find to choose among.

So give up same old, same old
one linguistic type of sandwich.
It's time to go more global
and to learn a fryin' language.

MRS. MARTINEZ'S FRYIN' PAN

Mrs. Martinez's fryin' pan has seen almost all that a fryin' pan can.

It's cooked up potatoes, tomatoes, and eggs.
It's fried some pancakes and once some frog's legs.

It fried a frittata and country steak twice.
It fried some bananas and of course some fried rice.

It fried up some shrimp and some noodles for dishes.
And also some catfish for Cajun fried fishes.

It fried up some beans then refried those beans.
And the very next day it three-fried those beans.

It's fried up some peppers, and onions, and 'shrooms
made fryin' aroma that filled up six rooms.

And the pan that fries up Oh so tasty a lunch,
combines with the genius of the Martinez touch.

So for ultimate eatin', and man that's no lyin'
see the pan and the Mrs. when they get to fryin'.

ROYCE THE WONDER DOG

Dad calls Royce the Wonder Dog,
but I never did understand why.
It seems like the Wonder Dog's some kind of title
That really just doesn't apply.

Royce is the king of the porch, you know,
as he lays his head on his paws.
His eyes are half closed, and his tail doesn't wag,
as an old bone sits in his jaws.

He doesn't move from his spot too often,
except to eat or drink.
He stretches and yawns and rolls out his tongue.
Once in a while he blinks.

And even though Royce doesn't do much,
lays around all day like a log.
Whenever Dad talks about that hound,
he still calls him the Wonder Dog.

So I asked my Dad, "with Royce that lazy,
and always so tired and tame
how come the addition of Wonder Dog
is tacked on along with his name?"

Dad said "you know some dogs can jump and run,
and some can perform in a show?
I wonder if Royce will ever do that,
or maybe just get up and go."

SPILLIN' REBECCA

Spillin' Rebecca just couldn't stop spillin'
any drink that was set at the table.
For all of her spillin' she wasn't not willin',
It seemed that she just wasn't able.

Early on as a baby, when she was sat down
to be fed in the kitchen high chair
no drinking container stayed upright too long,
what started out here wound up there.

For every meal this pattern continued
and for all of the nourishment spilt
her mom had decided that rather than fighting
its simpler to wash floors with milk.

There were cups and mugs and glasses and bowls,
any object in which you could pour.
Didn't matter the shape or the content or size,
eventually they all hit the floor.

Cider or juice, milkshakes or soup,
any liquid at all would suffice.
A bottle of water, a cup full of pop,
once a quart full of milk made from rice.

"Stop spillin' Rebecca" her mother would plead,
"have mercy on my floor and my soul."
After two years, then four years, and another three more years
she decided she must take control.

Her mother had tolerated all that she could,
reaching the point of no return.
"This spillin' is buildin' a need for solution,
there must be a way she will learn.

Then it struck her mom like a bolt from the sky,
to shut off the spillin' faucet.
The lesson that needed to be learned had to do with
connecting effect to what caused it.

So her mom said "Rebecca, it's time for a change,
from now on every spill that comes down
will be yours to deal with. And you can take care of
the mess that you leave on the ground."

Rebecca then suddenly found herself holding
a sponge, and a rag, and a mop.
And wouldn't you know it, from that time forward
she hadn't spilled one single drop.

I guess you could say that a miracle happened,
with such an immediate change.
Or there may be a scientific discovery
that someday research will explain.

Perhaps the story might offer a moral,
something about cause and effect.
Or maybe it's simpler, to stop all the spillin',
make the clean up her pain in the neck.

RUBBERT JOHNSON

Rubbert Johnson's got the knack,
if he's knocked down, for bouncing back.

Rubbert says "it's attitude,
that determines if you win or lose."

With first defeat, where most folks quit,
he'll find a way cause he persists.

And even on a rotten day
he comes up smiles anyway.

When miserable just seems to last.
You can hear him say, "this too shall pass."

And with an unkind twist of fate
he manages to bend not break.

When "can't be done," say all the experts,
no one could take that kind of trouncing.
Just watch one hundred per cent pure Rubbert
first hit the ground, then keep on bouncing.

DOC

Doc, I don't feel right. I think sumpthin's wrong,
'cause I look and I see only blue.
I'm sure there's a sumpthin' I'm sufferin' from.
So, tell me Doc, what should I do?

So Doc gives a listen and a poke and a prod,
and he says "stand on two feet, now one."
Then he scribbles some notes, and he mutters "ah, yes,"
then he says "here's the information."

"See, your tonsils are tensile, your kidneys aint kiddin',
and your gall bladder's gotta lotta gall."
"Your muscles are tousled, intestines are testy,
your brain's full o' rain, and that ain't all."

"When your feets hits the streets, with irregular beats,
there's no rhythm to your stride and your steps.
And your shoulders is over the place where your toes are.
You don't glide, you just shuffle and schlep."

"What you got's called 'the blues' and here's medical news,
you can turn this condition around.
Pick your head up and show off those nice pearly whites,
with a smile and get rid of that frown."

"Take those blue glasses off, so you can see clear.
Better yet, find a pair colored rose.
That's what you should do, and if I was you,
I'd buy two. Put 'em both on your nose!"

HOW ARE YOU?

Keisha Watson skipped through the field
of her grandfather's countryside farm.
She explored every corner from front gate to fences,
and all of the stuff in the barn.

There was one place she wanted to spend some more time,
at the old stone well, by the creek.
She was having a look down that long dark tunnel
when she felt that she needed to speak.

"Hello" she said, "hello" came back.
It surprised her to hear a response.
"Hey there" she called and "hey there" was heard.
A reply had come back more than once.

So Keisha worried, who's down at the bottom?
Are they safe, and how could she tell?
Then, her fear put to rest when she asked "how are you?"
The response returned was "I'm well."

SICK AS A DOG

I've heard it said about a man that he is:
sick as a dog,
happy as a clam,
smart as a fox,
strong as an ox,
eats like a bird,
stinks like a goat,
mean as a snake,
fast as a rabbit,
quiet as a mouse,
big as a whale,
pretty as a peacock,
crazy as a loon,
slow as a snail,
silly as a goose.
I thought I overheard one dog say to the other that his friend was as logical as a human. Funny, said the other dog, I would have said as passionate as a human.

MRS. WEISS'S LICE

Every kid knows that lice aren't nice.
So if you are smitten, take my advice;
see the salty school nurse, Mrs. Weiss.

She's conquered all those nasty critters
that find our heads and make us bitter.

She's searched and picked through every head
so much now that she's seeing red.

She'll grab one louse and keep on pickin'
those sons o' bugs, they'll take a lickin'.

It's misery once and worse yet twice.
But you know those bugs will pay the price
if they try messing with Mrs. Weiss!

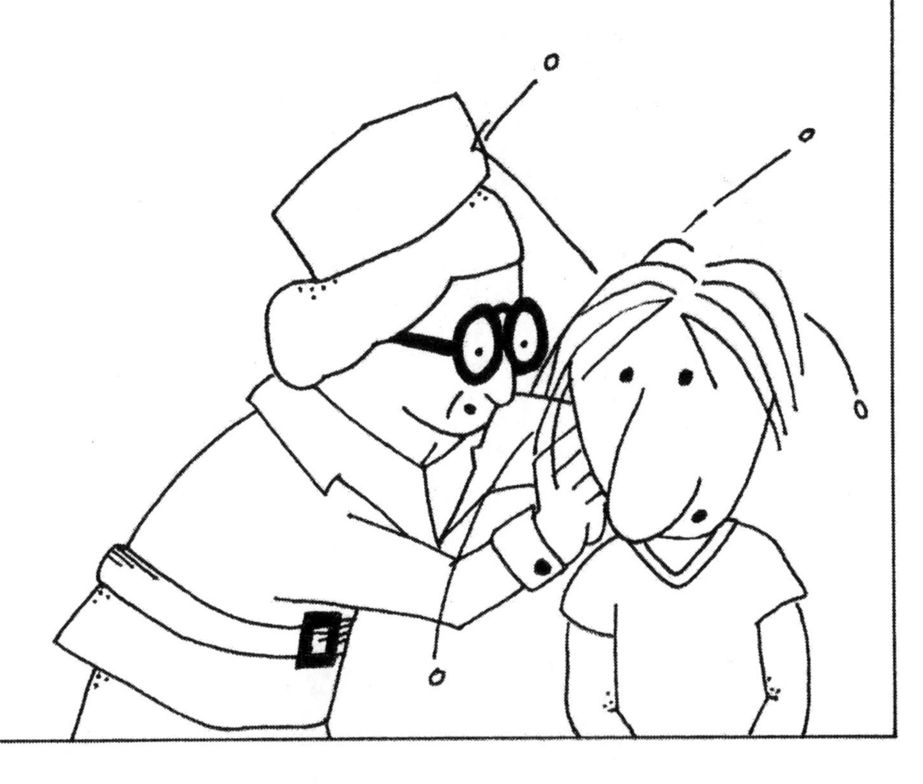

SECRETS OF ORGANIZATION

My teacher says success achieved
is a long term complex process.
But simple measures go quite far
to make the work load seem like less.

She says the most effective people
among the many girls and guys.
Are those that make the effort to
prepare themselves and organize.

The first of all the strategies is 2 learn how 2 prioritize.
Don't w8 4 1st concerns to just pop up and self identify.

There must be rULeS and guide   made to whicH one can adhere.
lines
Their definition and DIRect   should be nothing less than clear.
Ion

One need do**** away with {]</ clutter that serves #~(only to confuse.
And narrow down to ......bare essentials that you'll ``,, really use.

Recording all im_ort_nt poin_s is foremost in the pl_n.
Basics are to be laid d_wn and then the det_ils if you c_n.

The skill to compartmentalize creates utility.
It's waytoohardtomasterthings without divisionsyoucansee.

So organize your thoughts and things.
Then life that may seem so much harder,
won't really be so tough at all,
when out of chaos you make order.

BREAKFAST BRAND

Ever since I can recall,
a constant that remained
was our family's breakfast cereal,
that each day was the same.
It tasted pretty good, I thought,
as daily staple diet.
The "Holy-Os" that my folks bought,
didn't everybody buy it?

But one day someone told me,
on the supermarket shelf,
that I might find three dozen brands,
and check them out myself.
They said that I should scrutinize
ingredients and such.
To close inspect the packaging,
don't be afraid to touch.

Be sensitive to the appeal
of the icons on the box.
Know the companies that make it,
and who holds the major stocks.
And how is it consumed today,
and how it first it was made.
And know well all the rules by which
the offered games are played.

And so I did exactly that,
and as I ventured out
I went up and down the aisle,
seeing what this was about.
I found familiar "Holy-Os,"
but also "Righteous Crunch."
There were "Supreme Pops," "Almighty Flakes,"
and even "Sacred Munch."

There were smaller name varieties,
like "Holy-Moly-Os."
And slightly different products yet,
like "Holy-Roly-Os."
I was amazed as I discovered
the assortment that existed.
If I didn't take the time to look,
I'd otherwise have missed it.

Now I think I understand
why such a large selection.
Why folks like different products
that they find in the collection.
I've gained appreciation
for the brand I've always known
as it ultimately readies me
for a choice that's all my own.

ONE NICE GUY

My Dad said "let's get cookin' pal.
I'll teach you the fine art.
We'll make a feast like Bacchanal.
And you'll do the most important part."

"Now the first and foremost thing to know
is that you're happy when you cook.
And being aware that as you go
you keep the closest look."

"As I was saying, take a gander.
Observe me as I work.
Like Julia Child, her kitchen and her
recipes were all the perk."

"It's pure excitement choppin' veggies.
Notice my big smile.
The master chef knows in his head he's
joyful all the while."

"So, now it's your turn, take good care
as this is rather sharp a knife.
First you'll peel then cut the fare
then chop like it's the time of your life."

"And here they are. Six onions fresh,
for you to make your mark.
These are the biggest and the best.
Now hit 'em outa the park."

I started peeling off skin layers
and finished every one.
I said to my Dad, all smiles, "well, hey there's
cutting to be done."

And as I carefully cut large rings
my eyes began to swell.
I wasn't sure what this should bring.
I thought I was doing well.

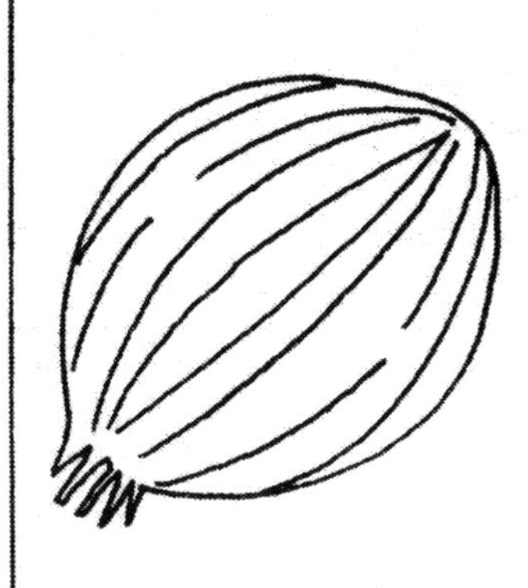

But soon the tears began to flow
well outside of my control.
Rolling down my cheeks, they'd go.
Dropping near the veggie bowl.

My Dad asked "why so sad there, friend?
What's going on that's got you down?
It seems the message that you send
is that the joy's gone out of town."

I said to him "but, I'm not blue.
I think you got the wrong idea.
I'm really happy, just like you,
even though I shed a tear."

So, Dad said "I can cheer you up.
This will bring those tears to stopping.
That stack of onions you built up,
well now it's time for chopping."

"Get in real close with chopping tool
so you can see each piece is right.
Then live the dream of 'top chef – cool'
and know chopped onions' rare delight."

I forced the smile upon my face
to let Dad know I'm happy still.
I chopped away at a vigorous pace
but once again, the tears did spill.

Dad said to me "I understand.
Perhaps today there's too much sorrow.
I know that you're a cooking fan
So, we'll try this again tomorrow."

Then as I wiped my face again
and cleared the blurring from my eye,
I knew my Dad's a caring man
and really one nice guy.

ANNA AND SAL

Anna's quite the quiet one,
in the middle of the class,
an ordinary any girl,
a steady stable lass.
While Sal is known for miles around,
always first in line,
she's always heard, always seen,
and always on the mind

Anna works behind the scenes,
to help with the school play.
Her role is fundamental,
though she hasn't much to say.
And Sal is just the opposite.
It's her face that you see.
At center stage she's all the rage,
that's where she's going to be.

In sports there's solid Anna
as she labors for her team.
She'll set up plays then pass the ball,
and always play it clean.
But Sal is always captain
and she's there for the big score.
She dances with her victory
so she can be adored.

There's constant recognition
if you're in Sal's company.
It's brighter lights and bigger sound.
It's be seen and it's see.
Not everyone's cut out to live
that lifestyle, constantly.
But you know Sal, she's always Sal,
she is Sal Lebrity.

For Anna life seems simpler
with the plain amenities.
It's do your work and pay your dues,
and then your time is free.
And most folks find they're comfortable
in Anna's company.
'Cause Anna's most familiar,
she is Anna Nimity.

POOTIN' PETE

Pootin' Pete refused to eat
the things that his mom said he should.
Like vegetables, fruit, whole grains and proteins,
that make up the good groups of food.

She said "don't you know, in order to grow
in a manner that's healthy and kind,
that nutrition's the key, so each day you will be
feelin' good from the front to behind."

Pete said "no sireee, that stuff's not for me,
I eat what I want and that's all.
Why care what the doctors and researchers say,
with my junk food I'm havin' a ball."

So for many a day Pete continued to stray
from a diet that's proven and sure.
Salty snacks and sweet treats were all that he'd eat,
"I'm not sick yet so who needs the cure?"

As the days and the weeks and the months all passed by
Pete hadn't slowed down one iota.
More cupcakes, soda pop, cookies and chips
and candy to fill the day's quota.

But the day did arrive that his zip took a dive.
He observed that he didn't feel right.
His stomach confessed that it couldn't digest
all the junk of a bad appetite.

Now Pete felt a rumblin' and he heard some grumblin'
from way down deep in his belly.
And that was the start of a legendary noise
and a product quite foul and quite smelly.

Well Pete was a pootin' a tune "rootin' tootin'."
He grinned and thought this could be fun.
But after a while he was losin' his smile,
his troubles had only begun.

Poor Pete didn't know, for how long this would go,
but he knew that he just couldn't stop.
Rapid fire was heard and the neighbors thought murder,
it sounded like someone was shot.

For each single stair was a rrrrrrrrip or a tear,
one so loud it broke sonic boom.
Some softer, some harder, this relentless farter
once got shot up clear to the moon.

As he slept and he waked his poor belly had ached
and the pootin' went on all year long.
Not only the noise disturbed girls and boys,
it was also the scent that was strong.

He cleared out two buses and people made fusses
'cause few folks could tolerate that.
His friends disappeared 'cause those who got near
got a whiff and dropped down to the mat.

Oh this poor pootin' fella, he performed a cappella
in a concert hall all by himself.
'Cause the chorus got wind that the orchestra thinned
and the audience ran to get help.

Now Pete had got scared so he then rarely dared
to eat much for fearing the worst.
'Cause he came to expect the next meal he'd select
would produce the next explosive burst.

Well he skinnied right down, to just barely a pound,
and then as it happened one day,
Pete pooted a poot, and then he went mute,
and ffffffffftt poor Pete pooted away.

So, what can we learn from the pages we turn
in the book of the food groups complete?
We should stick with good food, both young and old dude,
so we don't wind up pootin' like Pete.

WHERE THE ROAD SPLITS

Little Lauren skipped along,
as she went down life's road.
She walked and hummed a happy song
as was her normal mode.
It was her nature to look about
and take in what she saw.
To think about the hows and whys
that make up natures law.

But this day was a different day
as the road was taking course.
It approached a mountain, and she knew
you can't go through with force.
You have to take a path
that will allow you, in your stride,
to one way or the other
make it to the other side.

She stopped right where the road did split
and saw it went two ways.
She figured out that either choice,
after many days,
would get her to the same end point
on the mountain's other face.

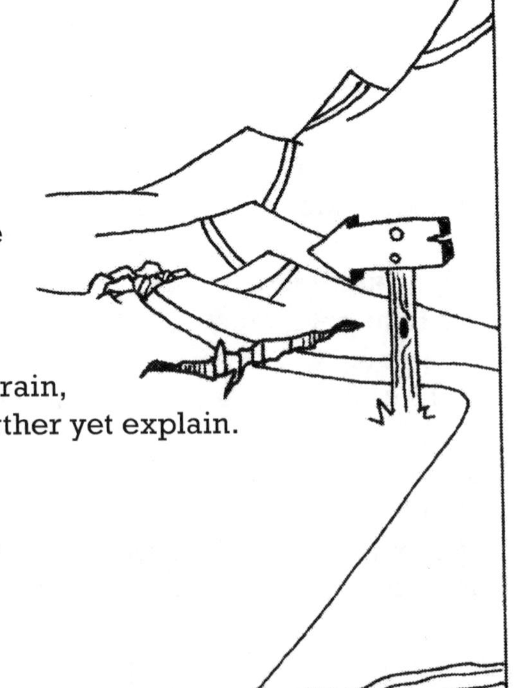

She watched with interest those that chose
the road to her left side.
The road had certain features there;
that she identified.
It seemed to be a newer path of riskier terrain,
that twisted sideways, up and down, to further yet explain.
It appeared there was a slope to it
with thorny bushes thick.
There were holes to fall in, mud to slip on.
And still folks took it quick.

There were people on this fast track
that had never done this tour.
They slipped and tripped and fell because
of footing that was poor.
What looked so hard was not at all
for those who well could see,
the ups and downs for what they were,
with road maturity.
For those who showed experience
with age that was time tested.
They went the road of obstacles
and some had even blessed it.

She studied then the other road
that traveled to her right.
She recognized its features
that were more familiar sight.
It still had twists and turns to it
though not as steep a grade.
A slower surer kind of way
that makes one unafraid.
She felt as if she knew this road,
the one of slower pace.
The young folks she saw go that way,
just didn't need to race.

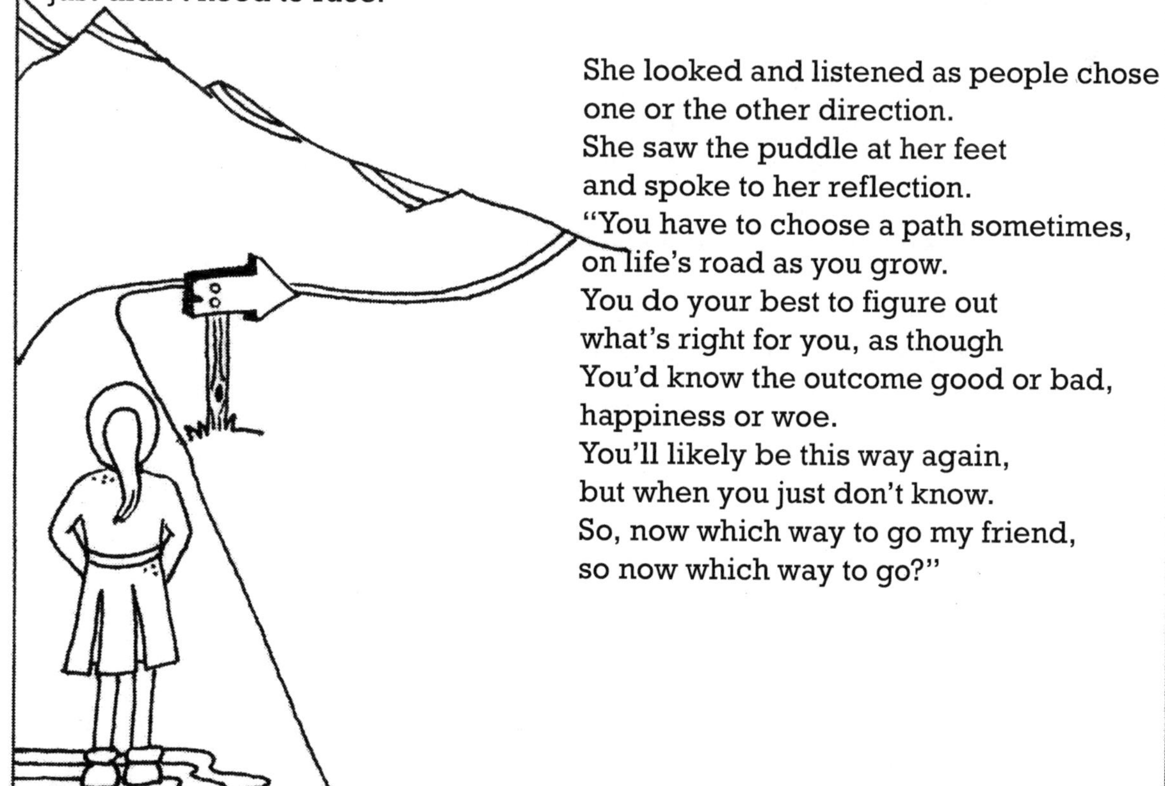

She looked and listened as people chose
one or the other direction.
She saw the puddle at her feet
and spoke to her reflection.
"You have to choose a path sometimes,
on life's road as you grow.
You do your best to figure out
what's right for you, as though
You'd know the outcome good or bad,
happiness or woe.
You'll likely be this way again,
but when you just don't know.
So, now which way to go my friend,
so now which way to go?"

FRASER DREW

It was his nature and his choice, therefore Fraser Drew.
He penciled his impression of the people that he knew.
He laid down his perception of the figures in his world
with lead and charcoal drawing tools on paper he unfurled.

The images were human forms in various positions,
as Fraser sought to illustrate complex and plain conditions.
He saw the outer person and would reproduce their form.
And drew out the inner person as believed was their true norm.

Round and oval polished stone of green and brown and blue
of different sizes, mixed with pebbles, in amongst the hues.
They made the form of a younger man digging in the soil,
a wooden shovel in his hand, the tool with which he toiled.

The children in a circle held their arms up in the air,
Their forms of fruit: apples, peaches, orange, plum, and pear.
Their faces showed the joy they took in game cooperation.
The different seeds inside their heads engaged in recreation.

Beneath a shadowy business suit of jacket, pants, and tie,
a see-through silhouette of man, and deeper still did lie
a kaleidoscope of broken glass, uneven edges sharp.
And polished diamond at the core, where otherwise a heart.

The coach's whistle in the hand that's pointing at the field.
The lower limbs were drawn in a collage of different wheels.
The torso was of solid oak and upper limbs of sapling branch.
The head contained both plans and notes penned previously by hand.

The mother held her baby close and higher to her chest.
Her female form of shiny steel beneath her feathered dress;
The baby's form contained both fluid and shiny silver tones.
Groups of minnows schooled about in newborn watery roam.

The woman's form was bent, as she relied upon her cane.
Her outline was of faded gold, and then inside the stooping frame,
dried up leaves of greens and brown, once bright red as a flame.
Lay underneath the clothing that said simple and said plain.

There were many more impressions that were part of the collection.
They best afforded medium for him to share reflection.
While never much for spoken word, but strong compulsion as he grew,
He recorded his experience, and therefore Fraser Drew.

BUSTED WHEEL

Last week I saw Bob Axlerod
sitting at the curb.
His head was hung as if to say,
I'm just a bit perturbed.
His skateboard sat there upside down,
I said "Hey Axle what's the deal?"
Pointing at his skateboard
he said simply "**bus**ted wheel."

And don't you know the week before
I saw him on his front porch step.
His lawnmower was on its side,
and I said "Axle what the heck."
"Weren't you supposed to get ten bucks
for cutting grass for Mrs. Teal?"
He said dejected "no ten bucks"
and pointed "**bus**ted wheel."

And wasn't it a month ago
I saw him coming down the street,
walking his bicycle right along,
instead of sitting on the seat.
I said "hey Axle why not ride,
just hop on and go for real."
He said "I can't" and pointed down
"I got a **bus**ted wheel."

So I feel bad for Axlerod
who right now seems down on his luck.
It seems that every time he starts
he winds up stopping, getting stuck.
And what's an Axlerod to do,
and how is he supposed to feel,
when every time he gets in motion
he winds up with a **bus**ted wheel.

BLACK AND WHITE

Frank Lee Black would hold his book
and read aloud the words therein.
"It's the black print on these pages
that defines what's just and what is sin."
"God said this, and God says that,
inside this book of precious pages.
And I know the true meaning of
those words that have endured the ages."
"Because I'm so enlightened,
in my righteous point of view,
I should say what people should
and what they shouldn't do."

Mark Ed White would hold his book
and "thump" it as he read.
"The white these pages offer
speak of grace and tell of dread.
God said that and God says this,
within this book of wisdom.
And I know true intention
in these words of grand theism.
Because I know the perfect truth
and see the one just way'
I should say what people may
and may not, day to day."

And in another neighborhood
a different book is favored.
The people there say that's the book
revealing God's true nature.
Mutluk Abiyad insists
the written words mean white as day.
And since he knows their meaning,
therefore folks should do as he would say.
Tehmamen Oswad says the words
in black are clearly proof
Only his interpretation
offers living laws of truth.

Frank Lee Black says "always black,
there's never an exception.
One need not think beyond the words
of clear divine direction."
And Mark Ed White says "always white,
in each and every case.
One ought accept that white's assumed
for all of human race".
Each one says the other's wrong,
that they and God are right
And they alone have answers
for the woes of human plight.

The book's the same, as are the words,
and yet there seems to be
completely different rights and wrongs,
depending through whose eyes you see.
I have to think who wrote those words
would recognize the chance
For people to review them,
and that they might be enhanced.
And with universal wisdom,
God would probably embrace
That one might think and choose in life,
as the world is a very gray place.

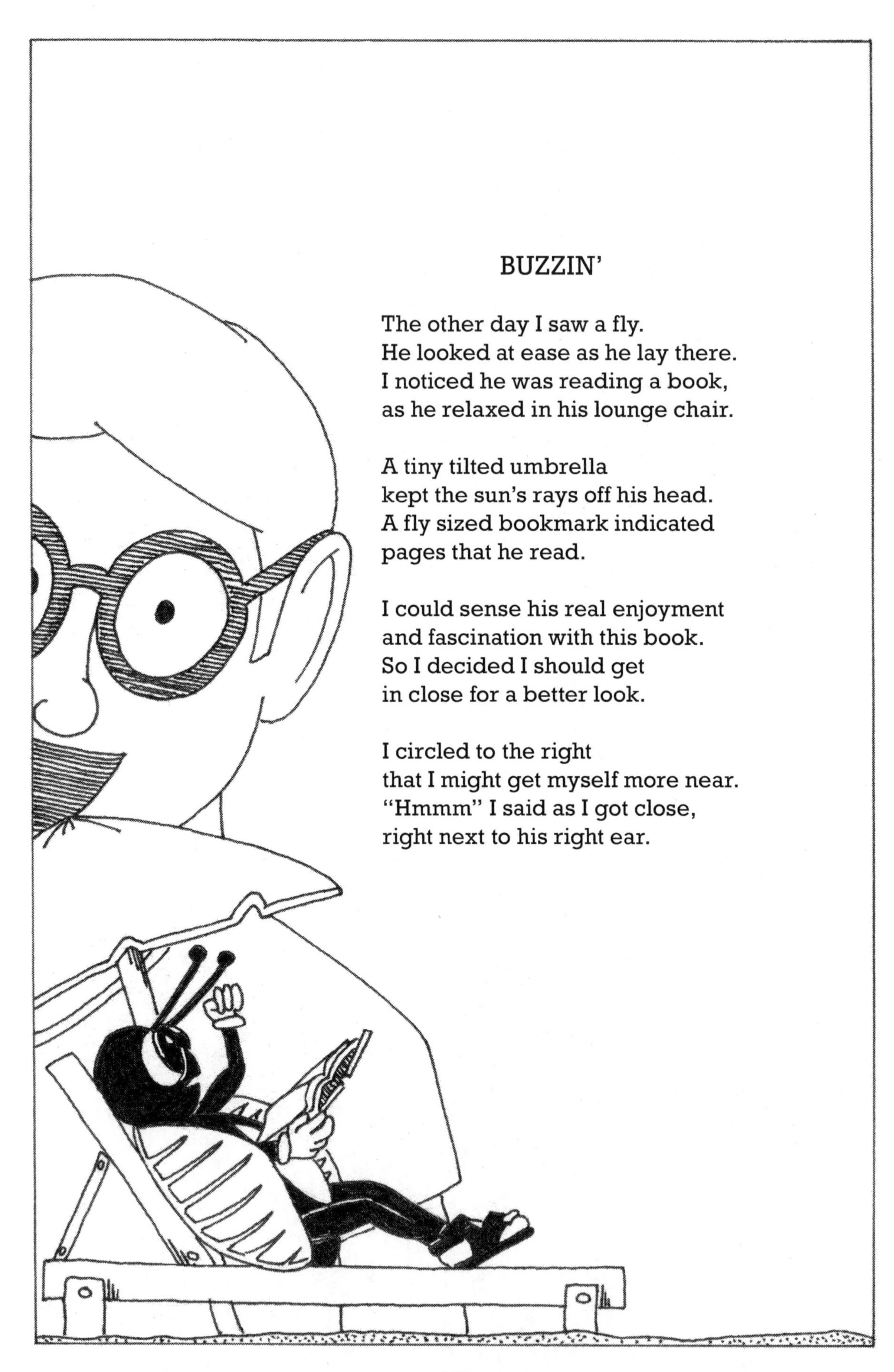

BUZZIN'

The other day I saw a fly.
He looked at ease as he lay there.
I noticed he was reading a book,
as he relaxed in his lounge chair.

A tiny tilted umbrella
kept the sun's rays off his head.
A fly sized bookmark indicated
pages that he read.

I could sense his real enjoyment
and fascination with this book.
So I decided I should get
in close for a better look.

I circled to the right
that I might get myself more near.
"Hmmm" I said as I got close,
right next to his right ear.

That seemed like it disturbed him,
as he flapped some his right wing.
"Hmmm" I said again, up close.
I couldn't read a thing

So to the left I circled,
that I might get the better glance
at what makes good fly reading
and what was there in those fly hands.

"Hmmm" I said once more,
as I had buzzed by his left side.
I'm just so curious, I gotta know
so, "Hmmm" again as I tried.

And this time the fly flapped his left wing,
as if to say "leave me alone."
He seemed annoyed when all I wanted
was just to say "hey" and have fun.

I kept trying different angles
with the hope of a better view.
He kept turning away and moving his book,
so what was I to do?

Eventually the fly had settled down
like everything's all O.K.
And then he ignored me, like I wasn't even there.
So, I got up and just went away.

ETIQUETTE ON ICE

Rumor has it hockey is a crude and violent sport.
When really looking closely, you see nothing of the sort.

The gentlemen of hockey, they are proper and refined.
Their manners are most elegant, their words are always kind.

It's "after you," "no, after you," "oh please I must insist."
Indeed one of the staples of the game is to assist.

There's mutual admiration and for rules complete respect.
"How do you do?" and "How are you?" They personally connect.

Their dress is most impeccable, matching shirts and socks.
Gloves to keep their hands clean and helmets on their locks.

They're courteous and polished and they're ever so polite.
Pinkies up when holding cups of tea at center ice.

So, contrary to images of edgy brawlers with cold hearts,
The atmosphere's civility for patrons of the skating arts.
And deep affection for the refs, regard for their respective part.
It's only when the puck is dropped that then the mayhem starts.

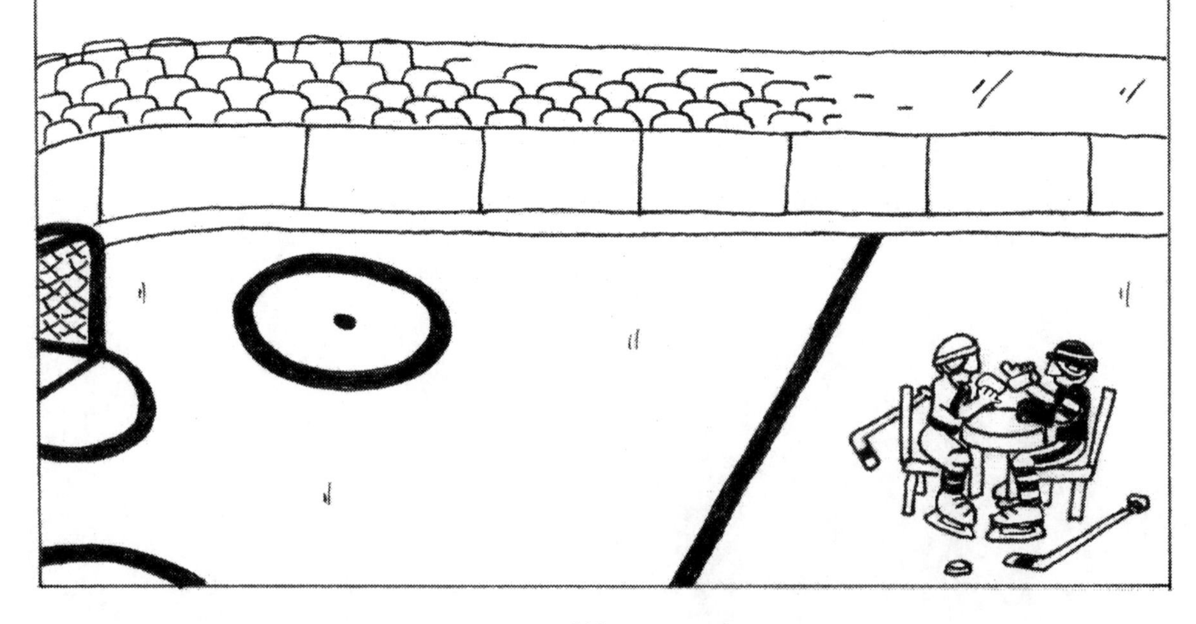

POLYTICKLE

Again the time had come around when people make a choice
of who will act as leader, and will give the people voice.
They hold the polytickle so that all who wish may hear and read.
That folks might judge the deeds and words of those who want to lead.

The first one said "my blah blah blah is such that blah blah blahs.
And I'll deliver, based upon the blah blah blah that was.
So if you cast your vote for me, together we will blah.
And show the world who's right because we are the blah blah blah."

The second one said loudly, "bloody blahdy bliddy blah.
My opponent says his blahdy blah will make your life more blah.
That's just a bunch of blankety blahbity, bumdity, blah blah blah.
And that's why you should vote for me, 'cause I'm your blah blah blah."

The next to go said "You should know that I have blah blah blahed.
And while the facts and figures show that blah blah blah seems odd,
the thinking person's choice is me, with my record of blah blah blah.
So vote for me, I'll guarantee blah blah da ditty blah."

The last to speak said sweetly "itty bitty blah blah blah.
We must consider everyone when we do blah blah blah.
So if you care blah blahty blah, well then your choice is clear.
Your vote for me helps to preserve the blah blah we hold dear."

The crowd in attendance cheered wildly, "yes give us more blahdy blah."
We're hungry and tired. It is you we admire with your brand of blahbity blah.
We can't get enough of this blah blah stuff. We really want so to believe.
It's the most convincing of blah blah blah. Surely you would not deceive."

Having listened to the polytickle and all of its blah blah blah,
The people picked and chose the most appealing blah blah blah.
So, with their votes collectively selecting blah blah blah,
they made their choice and set their course, accepting blah blah blah.

TEARS OF JOY

My mom said "sit down next to me,
and I'll explain how the wedding goes."
I watched how the rest of the guests arrived
and filled up the chapel's rows.

Then music started, and two kids my age
were first to walk down the aisle.
Everyone watched as they slowly walked by,
their faces showed big happy smiles.

Still more people walked down the aisle
to the stage where they smiled and stood.
Then some guy talked to the two folks up front
and that seemed to change the whole mood.

I heard him say something about "better or worse,
to have and to hold" and "do you?"
He asked them something about "love and to cherish."
Both of them answered, "I do."

He said "I pronounce you..." and that's when it started.
It's beyond me to figure out why
every old person needed a hand or a tissue,
to wipe away tears from their eyes.

I asked my mom, "was that a good or a bad thing?
Are you older folks happy or sad?"
She said "I'm so happy, and everyone else is,
we're all so incredibly glad."

"So why all the crying and tissues and tears?
It looks like you guys are upset?"
She said "we're so pleased. These are tears of joy
and we couldn't be happier yet!"

"So, all of this crying means you're really quite happy,
if my understanding's correct.
And all of you really are filled with great joy,
and that's about as happy as it gets?"

She said "That's right, do you understand now?
Is all of this making some sense?"
I said "I think so. And I've learned something new,
from all of this set of events."

When next I hear someone laughing out loud,
I'll pity that person I see.
'Cause I'll recognize that they couldn't hold back
all their sadness and deep misery.

OUR GARDEN

You could say that our garden is most unique.
It's really unlike all the others.
We've planted the plants that gardeners seek,
that can generate dozens of flowers.

There are flowers of spring like the tulip and crocus
for beautiful beds of display.
There are delicate flowers of summertime focus,
roses, petunias, and lilies of the day.
And the fall brings us marigolds, black eyed susans
and various types of mums.
In the entire gardening season
there's a colorful continuum.

But, our garden is different, not for the flowers.
That isn't how nature would have it.
A large patch of green stems, on which the rain showers
and in the center, one fat happy rabbit.

REFLECTION

Mom scolds me if I leave a mess in my room,
but in the sink there's last night's dinner plates.
Dad tells me I can't be so slow in the morning,
but he complains that each day he runs late.

Mom yells at me if I throw a tantrum,
but she'll slam the door if she's upset.
Dad hollers at me "don't be touching my things"
but kicks my toys on the floor that I've left

These things they see, that are so bad, in me, are they just meant for me to hear,
or...
is this really their opportunity to be screaming at the mirror?

THE SOMEDAY LIST

My uncle's got a list of things
that he's been getting to,
some things to see, some things to get,
and also some things to do.
He says that it's his "someday list"
and slowness ain't no crime.
"I'll be getting' to it all,
when I find the time."

He says he'll travel 'round the world,
on boats and planes and trains.
He'll someday visit famous cities
with the strangest sounding names.
He wants to try exotic foods
from all the far off lands;
dishes of Africa, Europe, and Asia,
prepared by local hands.

He says he's gonna get the parts
to fix up his old car.
And roll up all the pennies
he's collected in a jar.
He plans to someday organize
the entire basement stash.
And clean the attic and every closet,
and really throw out trash.

He says he's also gonna lose
an extra fifteen pounds.
And exercise each day of course,
get fit by leaps and bounds.
Oh yeah, that pile of books to read –
he almost started number three,
and almost finished one and two,
"just need a little time, you see."

"Oh someday when there's time, you know."
It must be close to twenty years.
That he's been sayin' this and that
and fillin' up my ears.
It seems to me that having heard
the plans laid out in full report.
The someday list grows long my friend,
but the time it does grow short.

HYGIENUS, HYGIENUS

The books of Roman history speak
of the mighty empire's fame.
Recorded are great accomplishments
that are linked with past emperor's names.
Famous leaders: Marcus Aurelius,
Maximus, and Augustus.
The tales of their civilization
have impressed us and also taught us.

Perhaps it is well for us to study
a lesser known leader of Rome,
whose famous achievement still influences
the way that we live in our homes.
It was Bestus Hygienus who took a close look
and then put his nose to the air.
He decided that something had to be changed
with Rome's current state of affairs.

He said to his chief engineer, Fastidious,
"the streets of Rome have a stink.
I fear that our city has grown unclean.
Tell me sir, what do you think?"
"Hygienus, Hygienus, the streets are a mess
with filth that covers each stone.
They're poorly groomed, they're dirty and smelly,
and so are the people of Rome."

Hygienus then said "Fastidious my friend,
given all that we've smelled and we've seen.
I command you assemble your best engineers,
that Romans and Rome may get clean.
We shall build a pipeline bringing water to Rome
for its buildings and the streets that run through her.
It shall carry away all the garbage and waste,
and that we shall call a sewer."

Fastidious said then "That's good for the streets,
but what shall our citizens do?
They will get even worse, sitting in water
that's running with pee and with poo!"
Hygienus declared "Let the cleanest of water
go first in particular path,
to a tub in the home of every Roman.
We'll call it the Roman bath."

"There, Romans may bathe and clean themselves,
and wash their dirt away.
They may look good and smell good and feel even better
on any weekend or weekday."
So Hygienus created the bath, as we know it,
increasing Rome's grandeur and glory.
Which reminds me of Hygienus's first cousin, Soapus,
but that's yet another story.

PHILOSOPHER

My parents keep complaining,
it seems like every day.
"Make your bed, pick up your clothes,
you never put anything away!"

So I sat down and thought about
this room cleaning concept.
I tried to blend their wants with how
my bedroom had been kept.

And when I considered maybe,
I should just do as they say.
I thought, philosophers would think this through,
and reason rule the day.

It would appear that in the world,
anything could be anywhere.
And so it follows, logically,
that nothing is nowhere.

If nothing is nowhere then everything is somewhere.
That seems pretty simple to me.
So then nothing having no place, everything is someplace.
I'm pretty sure on that we'd all agree.

It then makes sense that everything
has its own individual space.
And if that's so then it should go
that everything has its own place.

If everything already has its own place,
and that's how it was meant to be
Then all the stuff in my room's in its place,
now that makes just fine sense to me.

So I think I'll pick up a good book and read,
put my feet up upon my bed.
When my parents come back in my room, I'll tell them
what I figured out in my head.

That reason and thought have shown me the way
to a just and clearer vision.
There's no need to clean up what's right in its place.
See the logic in that decision?

SLEEPING AT THE EDGE OF THE BED

Sleeping at the edge of the bed,
it's a delicate balancing act.
It's the place between waking and dreaming
where fantasy dances with fact.

One could wind up falling, perhaps do some floating.
It's hard to say where this may go.
There could be a comfortable spot on the floor.
Or fly over miles like a crow.

It seems like such a swift journey
to the place between here and there.
The possibilities are endless
when the mind is permitted to dare.

And the children, they're comfortable resting
at the edge between later and then.
Between those times, no boundaries are set
before they are women and men.

There are those at peace with existing
in the time between future and past.
They want only to know that the edge is OK
and to visit is all that they ask.

M & P

I hope you get the messages
as you read through the passages,
that tell of human passages
which offer up life's messages,
so that generation's messages
are handed down through passages.